Center for
Creative Leadership

leadership. learning. life.

ABOUT THE CENTER FOR CREATIVE LEADERSHIP

The Center for Creative Leadership is an international, nonprofit, educational institution whose mission is to advance the understanding, practice, and development of leadership for the benefit of society worldwide. Founded in Greensboro, North Carolina, in 1970 by the Smith Richardson Foundation, Inc., the Center is today one of the largest institutions in the world focusing on leadership. In addition to locations in Greensboro; Colorado Springs, Colorado; San Diego, California; and Brussels, Belgium, the Center maintains relationships with more than twenty network associates and partners in the United States and abroad.

The Center conducts research, produces publications, and provides a variety of educational programs and products to leaders and organizations in the public, corporate, educational, and nonprofit sectors. Each year through its programs, it reaches more than twenty-seven thousand leaders and several thousand organizations worldwide. It also serves as a clearinghouse for ideas on leadership and creativity and regularly convenes conferences and colloquia by scholars and practitioners.

For more information on the Center for Creative Leadership, call Client Services at (336) 545-2810, send an e-mail to info@leaders.ccl.org, or visit the Center's World Wide Web home page at http://www.ccl.org.

Funding for the Center for Creative Leadership comes primarily from tuition, sales of products and publications, royalties, and fees for service. The Center also seeks grants and donations from corporations, foundations, and individuals in support of its educational mission.

Center for
Creative Leadership

leadership. learning. life.

Robert J. Lee
Sara N. King

Discovering the Leader in You

A GUIDE TO REALIZING YOUR PERSONAL LEADERSHIP POTENTIAL

JOSSEY-BASS
A Wiley Company
San Francisco

Center for
Creative Leadership

leadership. learning. life.

Jossey-Bass books and products are available through most bookstores. To contact Jossey-Bass directly, call (888) 378-2537, fax to (800) 605-2665, or visit our website at www.josseybass.com.

Substantial discounts on bulk quantities of Jossey-Bass books are available to corporations, professional associations, and other organizations. For details and discount information, contact the special sales department at Jossey-Bass.

Printed in the United States of America.

Library of Congress Cataloging-in-Publication Data

Lee, Robert J.
　Discovering the leader in you : a guide to realizing your personal leadership potential / Robert J. Lee and Sara N. King.—1st ed.
　　　p. cm.
　"A joint publication of The Jossey-Bass business & management series and The Center for Creative Leadership."
　Includes bibliographical references and index.
　ISBN 0-7879-0951-3 (hard : alk. paper)
　1. Leadership. I. King, Sara N. II. Title. III.
Jossey-Bass business & management series.
　HD57.7 .L439 2001
　650.1—dc21

FIRST EDITION
HB Printing　10 9 8 7 6 5 4 3 2 1

A JOINT PUBLICATION OF
THE JOSSEY-BASS
BUSINESS & MANAGEMENT SERIES
AND
THE CENTER FOR CREATIVE LEADERSHIP

CONTENTS

Preface   xi

The Authors   xvii

ONE Where Does Leadership Fit in Your Life?   1

   Did You Choose a Career in Leadership?   2

   Focus on Five Significant Areas   9

   An Ongoing Process   11

   What's to Come   12

   The Exercises   14

   Summary and Synthesis   14

TWO Consider the Current Realities and Expectations   17

   How Organizations Are Changing   18

   What the Changes Mean for Leadership   20

   Expanding Views and Images of Leadership   21

   Costs of Leadership   26

   Summary and Synthesis   29

THREE Ground Your Leadership Vision in Personal Vision   31

   Personal Vision and Its Connection to Leadership   31

   Exercises to Clarify Your Personal Vision   36

   Your Leadership Vision   50

   Summary and Synthesis   53

FOUR Base Your Leadership Values on Personal Values   55

   Vision, Values, and Behavior   55

   Understanding Your Core Values   58

   Values, Conflicts, and Careers   66

   Summary and Synthesis   69

FIVE Get to Know Yourself as a Leader   71

    The Importance of Self-Awareness to Leadership   72

    Your Personal Leadership Profile   74

    Your Motivation to Lead   75

    Your Leadership Competencies   80

    Your Leadership Roles   83

    Your Personal Characteristics   85

    Your Capacity to Learn and Your Learning Styles   88

    Your Responses to Change   92

    Career History and Lessons Learned   96

    Summary and Synthesis   99

SIX Balance Your Work Life and Your Personal Life   101

    The Importance of Balance to Leadership   101

    Interactions Between Work and Other Areas   105

    Balance, Mastery, and Parenting   106

    Achieving Balance   110

    Beginning to Balance   118

    A Continuous Process   132

    Summary and Synthesis   133

SEVEN Take Steps Toward Self-Aware Leadership   135

    Summarizing the Relevant Facts   135

    Finding Patterns and Labeling Themes   137

    Choosing Bell Ringers   138

    Weighing Costs and Benefits   140

    The Leadership Decision Ladder   143

    Next Steps   147

    Getting the Help You Need   148

    Summary and Synthesis   151

Appendix A: Program Participant Questionnaire   153

Appendix B: Leadership Resources   155

References   161

Index   165

PREFACE

Over the years, we have had the privilege of working with a large number of executives and young managers, most with high levels of achievement and potential. Too often, however, we have found they don't feel comfortable with the leadership aspects of their careers. Sometimes they aren't clear about what they should be doing or where they should be heading; sometimes they are frustrated, conflicted, or downright unhappy. Typically, they can't put their finger on a reason. They simply feel that something isn't right.

We have concluded that this malaise often exists because although people have not stopped to evaluate what being a leader means to them personally, they have assumed greater leadership roles over time. Rather than taking charge of their choices, they've drifted into their leadership careers. In some cases the drift is *away* from leadership roles without knowing the reason. And at times they've found that "things have changed"—what was obvious at an earlier age is no longer obvious.

For those just now getting onto a leadership track, the anxiety is that a leadership decision, either for or against, is being made by default rather than by decision or passion, and there doesn't seem to be a good way to objectively assess the match.

In our years at the Center for Creative Leadership and in career-counseling situations, we have seen that not addressing such concerns can be risky for these individuals and can also have negative implications for their families, co-workers, and organizations. People who hold leadership roles but lack the excitement, vision, and energy to go with the job are likely to cause problems for everyone, especially themselves.

What a waste that a significant number of people are sitting on the sidelines of the game rather than taking on leadership roles or full careers that would nourish them and add much to their organizations.

LEADERSHIP AS A DELIBERATE PERSONAL DECISION

Discovering the Leader in You provides executives, managers, and potential leaders with a way to examine leadership commitments and opportunities in light of broader life goals and aspirations. Its aim is to help you gain personal insight into what leadership means in the context of your own life. In our experience, this awareness gives you the ability to exercise more control over your career choices relative to leadership and to achieve greater personal success as a leader.

The book reflects our conviction that many people would benefit from a conscious, systematic approach to understanding how personal vision, values, skills, and other characteristics match up with leadership requirements. For the first time, a system is available for dealing with leadership as a conscious career decision, *an adult vocational choice,* rather than just a coincidental outcome of moving up in one's profession. We offer a way to examine carefully what may be making executives and high-potential managers uneasy or less than completely confident about leadership roles.

OUR INTENDED AUDIENCE

Not every leader or potential leader needs to read this book. People who feel very clear about their paths—either toward or away from leadership—won't have an interest in examining these issues. We hope they turn out to be right in their decisions and never have to give the matter another thought. Some folks are lucky that way.

Our experience suggests that the vast majority of people are operating in between the extremes on this dimension. Even if they feel reasonably good about their choices, they will benefit from checking out what's behind their intuitive reactions. Or they may feel uneasy and eager to find the better path. This book is for them.

We believe that what we have to say will benefit not only executives who have years of leadership experience but also individuals just now considering leadership as a career direction. Individuals participating in leadership development activities will find the book very relevant, either before, during, or afterward.

People who would love to get time with a career counselor or coach will find this book on target, although not a replacement for an experienced professional. If a good mentor or adviser is available, we urge you to take advantage of the opportunity. This book can help those discussions along.

We hope that leadership developers and career coaches also read this book. We believe it will help them help others.

Finally, we hope that this book reaches people who have not been seriously considering leadership roles. We strongly believe that leadership potential is very widely distributed in all cultures. Leadership must not be restricted to a limited slice of humankind—there's too much leadership work to be done, and it's too important to leave it to a few stars. We feel the world will be a better place when leadership fits into more lives.

THE FRAMEWORK

The book is designed around a systematic framework that connects "the inner you" to current or prospective leadership roles. We stay largely with the personal side of leadership, although the outside world is included in general terms. The intended outcome is that you will be clearer about who you are and who you want to become and thus more decisive about your leadership choices, happier with them, and more effective in acting on them.

How, then, to organize a reasonably comprehensive yet direct and workable search of this massive terrain? Here is where our personal experience has played the biggest role. Through lengthy discussions with each other and with colleagues, we distilled the essence of thousands of conversations over our own professional lives to come up with our best answer.

Our answer takes the form of a few key topics organized into a framework, accompanied by numerous thought-provoking exercises with specific and often highly personal questions to focus you down to your essential needs and desires.

The framework of the book is based on five key topics:

1. The *context* in which you are now operating, in terms of leadership roles, expectations, and opportunities.

2. *Your personal vision* and whether leadership is an important part of it.

3. *Your core values* and how they are related to your leadership vision.

4. *The personal qualities* that support your work as a leader and how they give your work its own distinctive style.

5. The *balance* between your leadership work and other aspects of your life and whether they give you adequate *focus, support, and energy.*

Chapter One discusses the problem of drifting into or out of leadership and the value of becoming more personally aware of how leadership commitments enhance or diminish your overall vision and quality of life. Here is where the framework is introduced as the basis for the journey through the book.

In Chapters Two through Six, each of the five key topics is explored in depth, with examples drawn from interviews and from public lives. The chapters have many exercises to work through and learn from, although no one is expected to do all the exercises. The goal is for you to arrive at your own answers to the main challenge posed in each chapter.

Chapter Seven brings together your insights from the first six chapters, guiding you through a process of summarizing where you are in your leadership career and deciding where you may want to go from there. Appendix B offers suggestions for further reading on all the key topics.

ACKNOWLEDGMENTS

Many people contributed to this book. Our first thanks go to the thirty-two managers whom we interviewed in 1998 at a key moment in our discussions. Each of these generous individuals had recently completed an executive development program at the Center for Creative Leadership. Their insights were based on fresh explorations and were very helpful.

All authors stand on the shoulders of those who worked the territory before them. We acknowledge that debt. Anyone who has been to CCL has seen the world's largest library on the topic of leadership—not that we've read it all, but we've read a lot of it and know how much good literature is out there. The research continues, and always will, into better answers for emerging leadership problems.

We drew from many experts on leadership. Some are connected to CCL and others are not. Throughout the book we offer their views or findings, not to expound any one theory but to help clarify a point or help you come to an insight.

We received excellent assistance from colleagues who are adjunct faculty at CCL. They have independent practices as leadership coaches and organization consultants. Their contributions were especially welcome because they have their own perspectives and data sources. We are pleased to acknowledge the help of Robert A. Dickinson of Associates for Psychotherapy, LLP, of Greensboro, North Carolina; Catherine A. Jourdan, a licensed professional counselor in Winston-Salem, North Carolina; Amanda Mathis, an executive coach in Durham, North Carolina; Sam Manoogian, president of Executive Coaching, of Greensboro; Roger Pearman, president of Leadership Performance Systems in Winston-Salem, North Carolina; Joyce Richman, president of Joyce Richman and Associates, Ltd., in Greensboro; and Ernestine Taylor, executive director of A Healthy Start, Inc., in Greensboro.

Byron Schneider of Jossey-Bass has been our coach and organizer from the beginning. We are sure he would also acknowledge his very helpful staff and management, as we do. But we especially appreciate how fervently he promoted this project.

Helping us actually create a book out of our thoughts and papers were two very able writers, Alan Venable in San Francisco and Bernie Ghiselin in Greensboro. Thanks, guys.

There would have been no book, however, had we not had the true leadership of a person who never chose a leadership career. Marcia Horowitz's title at CCL is senior editor, but she's that and a great deal more. Marcia was our champion, writer, thinker, helper, and friend. She came very close to being our coauthor! This is your book too, Marcia.

September 2000

Robert J. Lee
New York, New York

Sara N. King
Greensboro, North Carolina

THE AUTHORS

ROBERT J. LEE is a management consultant in New York City working with senior executives on personal and organizational effectiveness. He was president and CEO of the Center for Creative Leadership (CCL) from 1994 to 1997 and is a senior fellow of CCL.

In 1974, Lee founded Lee Hecht Harrison, a career services firm that now has offices in more than seventy cities worldwide. He is a charter member of the Outplacement Institute. He has been adjunct faculty at Baruch College, City University of New York, and has been a director of the Human Resource Planning Society. He holds a Ph.D. in psychology from Case Western Reserve University.

SARA N. KING is director of open enrollment programs at the Center for Creative Leadership, in which over ten thousand people participate yearly. She has worked with many executives as a manager and trainer of various CCL programs, including the Leadership Development Program ®(LDP), The Women's Leadership Program, and Foundations of Leadership.

King joined CCL in 1986 as a research assistant for a project that studied executive women's career development in Fortune 100 firms. This resulted in the groundbreaking book *Breaking the Glass Ceiling: Can Women Reach the Top of America's Largest Corporations?* (by Ann Morrison, Randall P. White, Ellen Van Velsor, and the Center for Creative Leadership; Addison-Wesley, 1992, rev. ed.). King is currently a member of a research team investigating choices and trade-offs of high-achieving women. She holds a B.A. from Wake Forest University and an M.S. in educational administration from Cornell University.

Where Does Leadership Fit in Your Life?

As counselors and trainers of executives, we've noticed our clients expressing new feelings and patterns of thought in recent years. Many of the leaders we work with seem less sure that they've found the best place for themselves in the world simply because they have found a leadership position. Despite high levels of achievement, they often admit to a feeling that something isn't right.

From conversations and other interactions with many who have passed through our leadership training programs, we've concluded that the problem often is that they have assumed leadership roles without thinking through what being a leader means to them personally. Although they may feel that they are in charge of the daily aspects of being a leader, they have never carefully examined how their work as a leader derives from or serves their personal goals, values, and abilities. As a result, they feel uncertain about whether they're spending their best years doing what they really want to do.

Do you sometimes wonder whether being a leader is really worth your while, given all the other things you could be doing with your life? Are you finding that holding a leadership position is different than you anticipated? Do you feel uncertain about whether you were cut out for leadership? Are you a prospective leader who's wondering whether leadership is really where you want to be? In this chapter, we'll explore questions like these and explain how the rest of this book can help you resolve them on a personal level through structured sets of discussions, questions, and exercises.

In essence, this book addresses two main questions: If you find yourself in a leadership position today or hope to enter or reenter leadership in the future, do you have a vision of what you'd like your leadership work to accomplish for you personally as well as for your organization? And are your personal goals, values, needs, and resources such that your work in leadership can truly be both personally rewarding and outwardly fruitful?

DID YOU CHOOSE A CAREER IN LEADERSHIP?

Between us, the authors, we have nearly half a century of experience in assisting executives in the development of their talents and careers. In the past decade or so, more and more of our clients have come to us with questions about their place in the world of leadership and the place of leadership in their lives. Previously, they would come to us to help them understand their strengths and developmental needs or to grapple with issues such as how to become a more effective agent of change; how to confront structural problems in the organization; how to handle politics or difficult co-workers; or how to minimize the tremendous stress of executive roles. Then we began to hear more worries from executives about their *fulfillment* as leaders than about their *functions* as leaders. We heard them expressing more dissatisfaction with their work lives. Even when performing well in their work, they expressed reservations about not having control over the personal aspects of their careers.

Of course, we've wondered why such issues have become more common in recent years. Some reasons may lie mainly within the individuals. Has the human potential movement shifted many people's concepts of what constitutes a happy life? Is a new generation of executives demanding more personal meaning in their work lives? Have there been changes in career patterns or family relationships? To all of these questions the answer is most likely yes. Perhaps these changes at least account for a greater ability these days to articulate the problem.

There may also be external reasons. Has the task of leadership changed? What about recent structural changes in business? In today's flat organizations of complex, dispersed authority, there is a need for leadership at all levels, from customers and suppliers up (or across) through each team and group to the senior executive level. The demands of leadership arise in many guises, not always clearly signaled by job title or official status in an organization. A senior "analyst" discovers that her position involves encouraging other analysts to do their best work just as much as it does applying her own technical skills. A senior "graphic artist" finds that he is more often attempting to inspire good work in outsource artists than he is in creating images of his own. At all levels, individuals can and do become leaders by default.

We believe that this is one key factor: In all kinds of organizations, large and small, private and public, managers and executives often drift into leadership positions inappropriate to their values, nature, or abilities. Initially excited about new opportunities for leadership, executives often soon discover themselves in a new position in which they feel mismatched or unprepared. The thrill of advancement and the seductiveness of power have carried them along the fast track to unexpected and sometimes less fulfilling destinations.

Other executives have found themselves in uneasy leadership positions because of someone else's dream for them—perhaps that of a spouse or parents. Still other executives find themselves dissatisfied because they are underchallenged: their talents and résumés clearly qualify them for senior responsibilities that they haven't presumed to seek and that have somehow not drifted their way.

Whether underqualified, underchallenged, or in some other way miscast, many executives today feel out of place or misaligned with regard to the leadership demands and possibilities inherent in their current roles. We believe that these people would benefit by choosing more consciously the best times and places to assert themselves as leaders. We think that they should also spend some time asking how valuable the rewards of leadership are in their lives.

A Blind Spot

In 1998, seeking a better understanding of this problem, we conducted focused interviews to gather perspectives from thirty-two managers who had recently completed executive development programs. (See Appendix A for interview questions.) The interviews revealed that many of them had drifted into or away from leadership roles without conducting much of a conscious, guided evaluation of themselves as leaders. This was somewhat puzzling, considering that the programs that our interviewees attended were designed for people who wanted to improve their practice of leadership through extensive feedback and increased self-awareness. The individuals were thus a self-selected sample of managers willingly engaged in sometimes difficult self-exploration. Yet even in this group, leadership roles had been attained very often mainly through drift.

For example, we asked our interviewees, "Have you thought about a life plan around leadership? Was leadership a conscious decision?" In a few cases, the answers were yes; the individuals had indeed given much thought to themselves in leadership roles. The ones who had done this work seemed to us more self-assured. Some had chosen to move to the next level, and one or two were content to end their careers in their present jobs. In either case, they stood on solid ground.

For the most part, however, our respondents were stumped. They admitted that they had not given leadership per se the same consideration they had once given their technical specialties.

"Well, I guess not," said one manager. "I don't even give it a second thought. You know, it's like you just try to get through each day and do the best you can."

Another admitted that he "fell into" his position. Another told us, "If I start getting crazy, that would help me make a decision. You know, if my life started spiraling out of control."

Overall, it confirmed our idea that there were few managers who had actively sought or were truly comfortable in their identities as leaders. We were struck by how rare it is for people in leadership positions today to have thought to any great extent about their careers as essentially careers in leadership. We were also concerned by how many interviewees were asking, "Is assuming the leadership role worth the effort?"

So we'd like to pose a few starting questions:

How much of your life today is about leadership?

Do you see yourself as a leader?

How comfortable do you feel in that identity?

Did you actually choose to become a leader?

Would you like to be more (or less) of a leader?

Do the benefits of leadership outweigh the costs?

The Problem of Drift

Many highly capable individuals have drifted into leadership roles. Organizational currents carry them upward, so that they arrive at leadership without ever having taken charge of their choices. A gap then arises between who they are as people and who they are as leaders.

Sometimes drift combines with a follower's frame of mind, as reflected by one executive we interviewed:

> The gentleman whose job I took two years ago at my current site—this is the second job I've followed him into. I took his last job, and I took this job when he left. We have this little parade going. [As for my next move,] I guess I'll just wait and see. That's really all I can do because the next job I really want was just taken over by someone recently; now that department is going through a major overhaul, and it'll probably be a good two or three years before she moves on and that job becomes open. She would be an ideal person to follow. She's a trailblazer in our organization. I want to be visibly aligned with her.

In other cases, the drift seems to be part of a general desire to "advance" in the organization, but the purpose behind the advance is unclear. One associate director with about twelve years' experience in business told us:

> I've been with [a large pharmaceutical firm] since college and have worked in several divisions with increasing responsibility. I got grounded in some HR, had roles as compensation and benefits analysts, and then got a generalist opportunity as an HR rep supporting one of our medical device businesses, and from there was promoted to associate manager and then was given an opportunity again as a generalist supporting our logistics. When we closed down some facilities and opened new ones, I had responsibility for that. Once that was done, I had gotten promoted to a manager position. I worked as a manager for a few years, took on additional responsibility for staffing, . . . then took on a role in productivity initiatives in our global group, . . . was the manager supporting that group, and then was promoted again [into the] same kind of role.

When asked how she knew she was ready for the next opportunity, she replied:

> It's usually when I'm bored. I'm into a routine, doing the same things, . . . not feeling challenged. You know, you tend to lose focus, you tend to procrastinate a little bit. That means it's time for me to move, time to start looking. [But] for the most part, I was not the driver. I was always [being promoted by supervisors or bidding on openings]. . . . Just this past month, my new boss came looking for me. I wasn't out looking for a job. It was a lateral move, again at the associate director level. I've been jumping around, you know.

One interviewee from an accounting background looked back on his career and saw status as a driving pattern:

> I've always felt I've been chasing titles. When I first started off in my business career, I was in a CPA firm. The highest level you could achieve was partner, so I was shooting for partner. After three and a half years, that goal did not seem attainable because the environment was static, [and] the economy wasn't growing. I'd have to wait for a partner to die. So I looked around to find the biggest and best [other] title, and CFO became the goal. I don't think I ever thought of leadership in terms of concern about other people. I thought they were all concerned about getting the titles, too.

Often the basic problem is that an executive position turns out to be primarily a position of leadership, rather than of the kinds of technical skills that played a determining role in elevating an individual into the position. Yet the personal implications of this difference may not be acknowledged. The result, quite often, is that even successful managers and executives grow uncertain. This causes a draining loss of effectiveness and a corresponding loss of commitment to career and organization.

The problem is real. Failing to address it can be destructive not only to yourself but also to your family, your organization, and your co-workers. It is a waste of your good talent, energies, and company resources if you are leading by rote, all the while experiencing an indefinable malaise that stands in the way of full commitment and fulfillment.

Oddly, however, the problem is still largely overlooked by organizations. True, "leadership" in general is a hot topic, and rightly so, discussed and promoted in a flood of journals, books, and training programs that has never been greater. At least one American university offers leadership as an undergraduate major, with courses in motivation, ethics, and systems thinking. Yet leadership is rarely perceived as a calling unto itself, a lifelong vocation as demanding as one's technical specialty.

This aspect of leadership is also overlooked by individuals. At some young moment in your life, you were probably urged to select and develop some area of technical knowledge, but you were probably never urged to select and develop leadership as a special skill or to decide specifically how leadership would fit into your life.

Not until they are in their thirties or forties do many managers confront the issue. By then, they have already made career decisions whose implications they can begin to understand only by sifting through mounds of personal feelings and information, much of it emotional, hazy, incomplete, and even contradictory. And no one offers a system or program through which to sort it out. Meanwhile the pressure and temptation to step into even higher levels of leadership are intense: the pay, the power, the perks.

The failure to weigh the rewards and costs and determine how leadership integrates with all aspects of life presents substantial perils. These affect not only the individual facing the choice but also the people the individual leads. With leadership comes tremendous responsibility for others. Poor decisions and poor fit can severely and negatively affect individuals who look to their leaders for answers. In his book *The Power of Purpose,* Richard Leider (1997) says that people want a "leader who is a source of vision and vitality and who can articulate a common purpose by which they can work" (p. 169). People who aspire to leadership must do so with clear thought and recognition of this responsibility.

We strongly believe there is great value in looking outward at the demands of being a leader today and concurrently looking inward to understand and discover the personal foundations needed for leadership and the likely personal rewards and costs of taking this path.

Stop for a moment to think about your career. At some point in your life, you probably knew and said that you wanted to be an engineer, nurse, retail manager, architect, information specialist, accountant, lawyer, or some other kind of expert. But did you ever say, "I want to be a leader"? If you did, you're rare. If you didn't, you probably moved unconsciously into a career in leadership without ever really examining how happy you would be in it. Try and answer these questions.

Apart from your technical expertise, have you ever thought much about your career as a career in leadership?

Do you think leadership could be a vocation unto itself?

Outside yourself, who around you currently depends on you for inspiration, guidance, direction, or other aspects of leadership?

To what extent do you think about leadership as a responsibility to others?

What does this responsibility mean to you?

Turning Drift into Conscious Choices

We are convinced that many people who are in or are considering leadership roles would benefit from a systematic approach to understanding how their personal nature and motivation align with their roles as leaders. As one executive noted, not many think about a systematic approach:

> I don't know how many people really plan their careers in terms of, "OK, I've got this, now I need to do that, now I need to do this so it looks good on my résumé." . . . I think we all come out thinking that because we're eager and willing and everything that it will be fine, that it will just take care of itself.

This book is for leaders and potential leaders who have questions, who are feeling unsure, or who feel they may have drifted into the wrong place. In many cases, leaders aren't aware of what's bothering them about their situation. Is it a lack of personal fit, a question of skill, a family issue, or a matter of personal style and character? What's the best way to sort this out?

In this book, we'll examine the personal side of executive leadership and offer a way for you to confront and deal with your questions. This examination will help you set a direction and limit your drift. It will help you reach the point where, to whatever extent you choose to lead, it will be a conscious, balanced, intentional part of your life. In other words, you will gain more control of your life. The process in this book will help you whether you have been a leader for some years or are just starting out in that direction. We've designed it also to help you whether what you need is mainly a bit of personal confirmation or more extensive support in facing a deeper personal quandary.

Knowing that most current and prospective leaders had never systematically looked within themselves and tried to match their vision, values, and personal assets to an often ill-defined leadership role, we've developed a framework for this process. We'll describe the framework and show how it can help you connect the inner you to your current or prospective leadership roles.

The framework integrates our experience with executives with ideas from colleagues both at the Center for Creative Leadership and in consulting practices. Accompanying the framework is a self-administered assessment process, which you can use to find out what you need to know about yourself in relation to leadership roles. By engaging in this process, you should reach a point where you can say, "I am just not suited to this work" or "Yes, this makes sense to me. I see how I can do this thing and grow with it."

This book is not a quick prescription for getting out of one leadership situation and jumping into another. It intends to help any executive—and anyone who helps executives—ask important questions about how to match and balance their inner passions with their outward executive roles.

Leadership Outside Work

Quite often during our interviews, managers spoke about their leadership roles only in terms of their jobs and organizations. Only a few included their leadership roles away from the office, perhaps as a single parent, community volunteer, fund-raiser, political campaign worker, or member of a rock-climbing club. For one executive, this is where her leadership development began:

> When did I start thinking about leadership? It probably dates back to the beginnings of my career, but not so much in my career work as in volunteer work. I took a leadership role in some of the volunteer work that I did at New York's Metropolitan Museum of Art, the Museum of Natural History, and other volunteer programs—just managing the situation, being responsible for different pieces, getting people to do things. I'm not sure I realized at the time that it was a leadership role. I think I just looked at it as something very organized. And something I'm really good at is organizing and being responsible for getting things done.

Although this book focuses primarily on questions of leadership at work, we urge you to keep in mind that leadership outside work provides wonderful opportunities, and many of the ideas in this book will carry over to non-job-related leadership. Leadership in family and community situations may allow you to try new skills, styles, and levels of responsibility. It often allows more flexibility in terms of the length of time you hold a leading role and how long you choose to do so. For some individuals who love to lead, the best expression of their values may be to remain primarily individual contributors at work and leaders in a non-work setting.

FOCUS ON FIVE SIGNIFICANT AREAS

The framework will help you organize your thinking and logically connect important career issues with leadership development activities. As shown in Figure 1.1, it is organized around five important topics:

1. *Changing context and demands.* What is the context of your current or potential leadership role? What special expectations and realities do leaders face today? What views of leadership prevail in your current situation, and what assumptions about leadership do you personally hold?

2. *Vision.* What is your own personal vision, and is leadership a part of that vision? Do you also have your own leadership vision?

3. *Values.* Are your personal and leadership visions based on your own core values?

4. *Self-awareness.* What personal qualities support your work as a leader and give your work its own distinctive style?

5. *Balance.* Do you have adequate balance and focus in your life, resulting from a good integration between your leadership work and other aspects of your life?

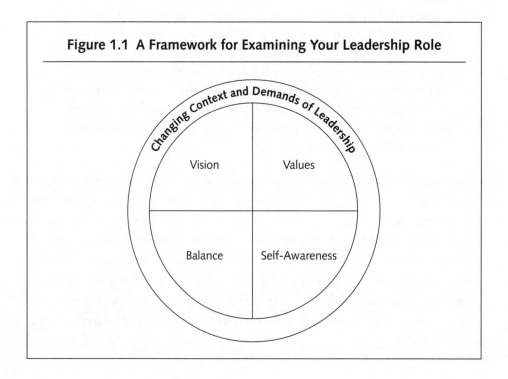

Figure 1.1 A Framework for Examining Your Leadership Role

Context and expectations, vision, values, self-awareness, and personal balance—these five topics frame the deep personal self-assessment that this book is all about. And we place special emphasis on vision because we find that while executives can usually articulate what is important to them, their leadership strengths, and their developmental needs, they often fail to recognize that these are all part of an overall vision. We believe that being purposeful about what you want in life is important to being purposeful about what you want in your leadership situation. Without an articulate personal vision, you will have a difficult time evaluating the leadership choices presented to you.

We also believe that everyone operates by a vision, whether they realize it or not. Recognizing and acting on one's vision is more than important: it's crucial. For some individuals, the challenge is mainly finding the time to uncover some fairly accessible truths. For others, it's a more arduous task.

The five topics are closely related. External realities and expectations provide a context for operationalizing your personal and leadership visions. Your values and how you play them out in your everyday life are the concrete representations of vision. Self-awareness, too, must be tied back to vision as a sort of catalyst, or glue, if you will. Does what you do reflect who you are and where you want to go? Similarly, your personal vision derives from the many facets of your life. Therefore, life integration is crucial, and life balance can only be judged in the context of your own personal vision and values. Because all of these concepts are related, a major theme in this book will be making more conscious, unifying connections.

This concept of five significant areas isn't new or exotic. Nor is our purpose to convince you that we've made the latest "cutting-edge" discovery in the science of leadership. This book is not so much about cutting edges as it is about the personal power that drives the blade. As Kevin Cashman (1998, p. 18) says, "We lead by virtue of who we are. . . . Whether we are at an early stage in our career, a knowledge worker, or a corporate executive, we are CEOs of our own lives."

AN ONGOING PROCESS

We hope to help you construct a personal approach that you can use now and also at a later stage in your career, not to push you into a change. In fact, this book might resoundingly confirm that you've already found a good path. Some people find that moderate-sized changes can be made right in their present positions or in their off-the-job lives, with important changes in attitude. Even if a major change seems called for, now may simply not be the right time. If, for example, you are carrying a heavy mortgage, you have two children in college, and you have considerable medical bills, it might be foolhardy to risk your current professional position— although even then in some cases the risk might be in order.

The framework *is* meant to help you discern an overall pattern in your work life that relates to a personal call to leadership. It should help you become aware of what's important to you and help you manage your career more actively. Perhaps when the time is right you can use this information to alter your circumstances. Deciding when that time comes may require using the framework at several future moments.

What you ultimately decide to do about leadership is, of course, your own decision. Choices depend on what's available, your level of excitement and discomfort, your chances to express yourself better in your current position or elsewhere, the supports at hand, courage, insight, and perhaps luck. There are no perfect outcomes.

WHAT'S TO COME

Each of the next five chapters covers one of the topics in the framework.

Chapter Two, "Consider the Current Realities and Expectations," looks at the changing context of leadership and changing conceptions of what leaders are and do. It's mainly about external expectations and realities. It discusses recent rapid economic and social changes that are affecting leadership at every level. It poses such questions as "What do you see happening out there in the turbulent world of organizations?" "What impact do these changes have on leadership?" and "What forces are shaping your current feelings about being a leader? Do they present opportunities for you to develop as a leader?"

Chapter Three, "Ground Your Leadership Vision in Personal Vision," explores the necessary relationship between personal vision and effective leadership. In the view of many, a person without a clear vision cannot lead a group or organization anywhere. The chapter will raise questions such as "Do you work from a vision that provides meaning, purpose, energy, and passion to yourself and others?" and "How does your leadership vision mesh with your broader personal vision?"

Chapter Four, "Base Your Leadership Values on Personal Values," asks you to inventory your values to see how they are currently reflected in your life and how strongly they serve as a basis for leadership. The chapter will also help you uncover any conflicts or disconnects that might interfere with your work in leadership. The chapter will raise such questions as "What are your core values?" "Are they realistic and reflected in your actual behaviors?" and "What other values define and support your work as a leader?"

Chapter Five, "Get to Know Yourself as a Leader," discusses the importance of being aware of your own particular skills and qualities related to leadership work. It leads you through an inventory of leadership competencies, roles, traits, learning styles, responses to change, and knowledge based on your business experiences. The chapter will help you pinpoint talents and skills where you show strength and others where you may want to improve. The chapter will also draw connections between your self-awareness and your ability as a leader to build trust, be flexible, and forge teams.

Chapter Six, "Balance Your Work Life and Your Personal Life," provides perspectives on the impact of a leadership role on the other aspects of your life. It suggests ways in which your life at home and at work can be mutually supportive. It asks questions such as "Do you look at your life as a matter of sacrificing time in one domain (such as your work life) in order to have time for other domains (such as family or community life)? Or can you look at it more in terms of integrating across different domains?" "Given your vision and values, what's the right balance or integration between work, home, and other interests?" and "How successful is your current balance? What might need to change?" The chapter provides some useful strategies for dealing with this difficult problem.

Chapter Seven, "Take Steps Toward Self-Aware Leadership," pulls together key themes from the earlier chapters. It gives you a process for integrating discoveries made throughout the book, culminating in a few key themes and insights that can clarify and drive any future decisions regarding leadership in your career. It will also discuss how to get help from colleagues, family, networks, and mentors.

Appendix A contains a copy of the questionnaire that we used to survey the thirty-two Leadership Development Program participants on their views of leadership and career. Appendix B lists books, articles, and instruments to consult for additional information.

THE EXERCISES

Each chapter contains numerous leadership-related questions and exercises that we have found helpful to executives. Not every exercise or question will be right for you, so be selective. But also be disciplined about tackling exercises that will challenge and stretch you. We've developed the exercises to serve a range of personal needs and styles. Give your major time and attention to the ones that work best for you.

You will get the most out of this book if you allow yourself the time not only to think about the questions that it raises but also to write down your responses. Writing is a way of sorting out your thoughts.

By writing down your thoughts, you will also prepare yourself to compare your current conclusions with new thoughts that you may arrive at in the future. Your ideas will certainly change as your career in leadership develops. A benchmark now may be useful to you in the future.

For some exercises, it will be possible for you to respond by writing your thoughts directly in the space provided on the page. You may want to make enlargements of some pages to give yourself more room to write. Or you may want to do all your writing in a separate notebook or journal. For some exercises, you may find it more convenient to type your thoughts. Record your thoughts with the method or combination of methods that works best for you.

Keep in mind that you are not simply following our line of questioning but developing your own, more personalized tool that can be useful to you at more than one stage in your career.

SUMMARY AND SYNTHESIS

Through systematic self-assessment, you can gain greater mastery over the leadership aspects of your career and your life as a whole. You can also overcome some of the passivity that has perhaps led you to a position of leadership that you never made a decision to enter and where you may now feel less than fulfilled.

This book will help you explore and synthesize ideas about the five closely related themes in our framework: external realities, vision, values, self-awareness, and balance.

If a leadership career is what you want, you'll benefit by becoming more aware of how your personal vision, goals, and other aspects of your life can enhance or direct your choices. You *can* master a career choice in leadership.

Respond to the following questions by writing in the space provided or in a separate journal.

1. What kinds of questions about leadership have you had?

_____

_____

_____

_____

_____

2. Are you facing any immediate decisions about your leadership role?

_____

_____

_____

_____

_____

3. How do you plan to use this book? How do you envision this book being helpful to you?

_____

_____

_____

_____

_____

4. If you are currently acting as a leader, officially or unofficially, what do you enjoy about it?

_____

_____

_____

_____

_____

5. What do you *not* enjoy about it?

_____

_____

_____

_____

_____

6. What thinking have you done about yourself and leadership as a career? What goals do you have for yourself as a leader?

_____

_____

_____

_____

_____

Consider the Current Realities and Expectations

This book deals mainly with leadership in formal organizations—small, medium, and large businesses; governmental and military agencies; professional, civic, and trade associations; charitable, educational, and religious systems, and so forth. Within these are, of course, teams, project groups, production shifts, departments, branches, offices, divisions, and subsidiaries—where most leadership is actually taking place. Leadership also occurs in other settings, and our discussions in this book apply to these as well. There are leaders on sports teams, among yacht crews, and in teachers' organizations. Volunteers lead scout troops, beautify neighborhoods, put on summer stock productions, and help with political campaigns. Leaders are active in all of these places, and nearly everyone has at one time or another had to decide whether to take on a leadership role.

In short, there's an organizational world out there that affects what kind of leader you can be, what you can accomplish in leadership, and how your role as a leader will affect the rest of your life and the lives of others. There are also commonly understood (and changing) views of leadership that surely have affected your personal views.

The first step in our framework is to look at this outer world as a context in which to envision leadership and the kinds of expectations it might bring. In this chapter, we'll look especially at how organizations and leadership are changing. Use this chapter to stimulate your own observations of these changes and their possible effects on you.

HOW ORGANIZATIONS ARE CHANGING

Nowadays we cannot define organizations as clearly as we once could. Many have become so diffuse and pluralistic that old static models no longer hold. Doug Miller (1997) depicts the organization as a chameleon, which "constantly adapts itself to its environment" (p. 119). Peter Drucker (1995) portrays organizations as inherently unstable because they "must be attuned for innovation, for the systematic abandonment of whatever is established, customary, familiar, and comfortable" (p. 77). All of the major changes we are experiencing can't be outlined in this book, but let's take a look at a few.

From Hierarchies to Customer Focus

A general shift has occurred from hierarchical forms to greater customer focus. Many years ago, when flappers danced the Charleston and what was good for General Motors was good for America, status and hierarchy were understood and accepted as primary qualities of organizations. This time of innocence was marked by a common understanding of assets, ownership, employees, bosses, and customers. Distinctions were clear. Organizations owned or controlled whatever they considered their business. Efficiency was a question of continuous high levels of production and sales that pushed volume beyond a fixed break-even point: the greater the volume, the greater the profitability.

But major changes soon took place. Products became more complex. Technological advances led to continuous change, faster communication, and new product lines. Assets became intellectual rather than physical. Customers began to have a more direct influence on the future plans of organizations.

As a result, organizations have now entered a highly competitive, quality-conscious environment where flexibility and responsiveness are paramount. Buyers expect more for their money and will cross whatever oceans, deserts, or Web pages may be necessary. They demand that products and services be customized. Rapid cycle time has become a major source of competitive advantage, and the lifetime of new products is often so short that the next version is gearing up before the last has fully rolled out. At the same time, organizations must do more with less as resources become more scarce.

These changes have led to a dispersal of authority and expertise, and a decentralization of power. As a result of the dispersal, companies once organized as pyramids now take on many different forms in hopes of achieving a structure that will best serve the customer.

Changing Careers and Employee Relations

Together with the dispersal of authority, employment arrangements have been changing. Today, some traditional business structures persist, but many new employee relationships are temporary or ad hoc. Organizations no longer have to employ all the people they need, let alone keep them in house and in sight. Partnerships, outsourcing, flexible labor, and interim managers are ways of keeping risks within bounds yet preserving the slack needed to cope with peaks or emergencies.

Accompanying these employment changes is a new orientation to jobs and careers (Hansen, 1997). Already apparent in the workplace is less emphasis on jobs and more emphasis on tasks and assignments. This will continue. Although workers will perform tasks, they will also need to create tasks. Everyone will be an entrepreneur. The location of work will change. Workers will conduct their work at home, on planes, in hotel rooms, and in other settings. More and more people will be "vendor-minded" temporary workers, changing jobs several times, looking for unmet needs and creating change.

"We are moving toward a network society rather than an employee society," writes Drucker (1997, p. 2). How work gets done and who is involved will reside largely in the hands of individuals and not traditional organizational decision-making structures.

Generational Changes

Major attitudinal changes have also taken place between generations. Over the past ten or fifteen years, we have witnessed major changes in people's willingness to respect formal authority. The shift began with the baby boomers, the generation born between 1946 and 1962. It entered yet another phase with the "baby busters," also known as Generation X, born between 1963 and 1981.

Now occupying the executive suites, the baby boomers saw authority crumble in ways their parents never did. They witnessed a failed war in Vietnam, the assassination of national leaders (John Kennedy, Robert Kennedy, Martin Luther King Jr.), the disgrace of a president after Watergate, and environmental disasters such as Three Mile Island. To this group, authority appeared unreliable and often just plain wrong. This generation's college years were marked by rebellion and protests unimaginable to the Silent Generation that matriculated in the 1950s. However, over the succeeding years, the boomers have demonstrated a strong work ethic and considerable loyalty to traditional forms of authority. Many of them have also placed the demands of work ahead of their personal lives.

The baby busters, so named because of the drop-off or "bust" in births following the baby boom, are the children of dual-career couples and of parents whose marriages ended in divorce in record numbers. With this generation, the adolescent idealism so characteristic of the boomers gave way to a more pragmatic and cynical realism.

Like the boomers, the busters possess a strong sense of determination and willingness to work. But this is balanced by a desire to keep work from infringing on their personal lives. However hard they work, they think as much about boundaries, balance, quality of life, and family as they do about organizations and careers.

WHAT THE CHANGES MEAN FOR LEADERSHIP

During times of more hierarchical structures, successful leadership meant setting and implementing clear plans. Middle management's roles were to ensure that fixed assets were efficiently employed, adequate sales levels were sustained, machine schedules were efficient, workloads remained high, and a general watchfulness was maintained. But as times have changed, so has the nature of leadership at every level.

First, to accommodate the needs for flexibility and rapid reactions to customer demands, organizations have had to decentralize and provide leadership at more intersections and more customer points; there isn't enough time to send messages back and forth to the executive suite. Furthermore, the people sitting in the executive suite may not have the detailed knowledge needed to reach decisions.

Second, organizations are requiring different skills of leaders. Leaders must understand complex issues surrounding the coordination of systems. They must continuously rearrange work routines, communication patterns, and performance standards. And they must be less concerned with supervision and "managing upward" than with coordination for the benefit of customers. Leaders must develop the ability in themselves and their staff to discern customer needs and to be innovative, responsive, flexible, and comfortable with ambiguity and change.

Old patterns of command and control are replaced by or intermixed with relationships in which no one controls and no one commands. More than ever, leadership is about influence rather than authority. The growth of alliances and value chains brings shifting boundaries where managers will be most effective if they focus on good relationships. Also, job descriptions have become less clear and therefore less useful in resolving conflicts.

Finally, generational changes in attitudes make a tricky job of defining and establishing influence and authority. Leaders today must bear in mind that younger generations will be less loyal to traditional authority than the boomers have been. They will not expect cradle-to-grave job security in a traditional hierarchy. They will work for three to five different employers and lose their jobs at some point. They will feel that their loyalty belongs to their teammates, not the corporation.

Managing this generation as the "boss" will only backfire. Conger's take on the role of boss is, "No longer a positive sign of accomplishment and authority, [the] term now symbolizes distance from others, an unreasonable toughness, and other not-so-attractive connotations" (1997, p. 18). Leaders will need to find new ways to motivate and meet the needs of this generation and the generations to follow.

Take a moment here to review these organizational changes and their impact on leadership. Think about what you yourself have seen going on around you.

How do these organizational changes manifest themselves in your particular organization and industry?

What implications have the changes had for leadership?

How have these changes helped or challenged you recently as a leader?

What further developments do you expect?

EXPANDING VIEWS AND IMAGES OF LEADERSHIP

A result of the changes just described is that there is less consensus today on how leadership is defined. We now have multiple definitions of leadership operating in a multitude of ways. Leaders are often harder to spot by their titles, and job descriptions of leaders may point toward a wide range of expectations for what the person in that job will actually do or the style to be used to lead.

These expanding views of leadership can be both motivating and daunting. The challenge is to understand their impact on your own individual views and images of leaders and leadership in the political, military, spiritual, or corporate realm. It's important to know your own views because those views affect how you think and behave in several areas, including making decisions about your career.

Seven Common Views of Leadership

Following are seven views or images of leadership that we frequently encounter. These perspectives are blends of fact and fiction, stories and experience—the received, unquestioned wisdom of a particular culture. Each perspective carries its own implications. Some are mainly about who becomes a leader and how. Others have more to do with how a leader should lead. As you read about these views, think about how they might affect your sense of yourself as a leader and the ways you interpret that role.

1. *The Genetic View.* This view holds that some people are born with leadership talent and others are not. Only certain people can learn to lead effectively; they're naturals. If you don't have this inborn talent, there's nothing you can do.

2. *The Learned View.* If you study leadership carefully and practice what you study, you too can be an effective leader, no matter who you are. In a sense, this is the opposite of the genetic view. Belief in the learned view is common in the military and among professional leadership developers.

3. *The Heroic View.* The only good leaders are those who perform courageous, wise, and benevolent feats that the rest of us can't. These are the movie roles played by John Wayne, Gary Cooper, and Jimmy Stewart. Leaders are the people who get the rest of us out of trouble.

4. *The Top-Only View.* This is the view that leadership only happens at or close to the top of an organization. Everyone else "just follows orders." If you're not the boss, you're nothing. If you are the boss, you're everything anyone could wish for.

5. *The Social Script View.* When it's your proper time to be a leader, you'll be asked. When asked, you should accept and be grateful. After all, not everyone is asked. Social scripts also create expectations about who is likely to be asked. The assumptions in our social scripts are the result of powerful influences from early family life and our surrounding cultures; their effect on us should not be minimized, even if they aren't easy to identify.

6. *The Position View.* If you're in the job and have the title, you're a leader. This notion is traditional in bureaucracies and highly structured organizations and carries some validity even in the most virtual of systems. If your title is phrased "director of . . ." or "head of . . . ," your leadership virtues are assumed.

7. *The Calling View.* Although not necessarily a religious experience, a "call" to lead can be quite compelling. It involves a deeply felt sense of mission, of private purpose, of inevitability. It might be so powerful that one has little sense of control. This calling isn't especially rational, but it is extremely personal. It is not for others to judge whether someone's calling is valid or appropriate but rather to accept that some people have this kind of insight and act on it. Equally compelling might be the absence of that inner voice. One might thus speak as Gen. Colin Powell did in 1995: "I don't find that I have a calling for politics. But I want to keep the option open" (Stacks, 1995, p. 22).

Each of these views is worth exploring and can lead one to unexpected places. Consider the last, the calling view.

For many years, Paul West (a fictional name) had felt a calling to help, to bring harmony, to help others see their potential as individuals and as a community. What he didn't know was how to make this happen. An early career in sales was disappointing: he made a living, and his products were honest and worth what they cost, but they didn't come close to touching lives. He left the sales force for the seminary and became a minister.

But the ministry didn't work for him either. To him it seemed too parochial and ritualistic, with not enough spirit and humanity. He accepted an offer from a nonprofit that needed a manager to run a unit that provided development experiences for people across the country.

Paul did well at this work. His staff liked him, and his preaching and counseling skills were useful. For a while, the world seemed fine. Then Paul found that this leadership role had become more about managing than serving. So at a time of peak effectiveness in his organizational career, he stepped away from running a department and became an individual contributor within the organization. He found that he could promote his deeply felt values more explicitly when he did one-on-one work than when selling and running programs delivered by lots of others. He found that he would rather develop relationships with a few customers of his choice than do superficial work with many kinds of organizations.

For now, at least, the world seems fine to Paul. We think it will stay that way for him. He's found a very comfortable and effective way to be the kind of leader he wants to be.

The various views of leadership are not mutually exclusive, nor do they presume to define your views or images of leadership, no doubt a blend of many ideas, sensations, and theories. A part of your perspective may be the result of having felt the call. Another might be the result of being thrust into a role, making the best of it, and doing quite well.

Our views of leadership are informed by our experiences with success and failure, gain or loss, trial and error. Each reinforces or modifies that view. All too often, however, we overgeneralize.

Results of the Differing Views

The differing views of leadership carry implications for personal choice and what is expected of you as a leader. In both of these areas, you're much better off if you're aware of your own views.

Implications for Personal Choice As we noted, the choice and awareness of views does matter: As an image or view dictates, certain paths and options will seem desirable and make sense, and others will not. Your images govern what you believe possible, what you are trying to accomplish for yourself and others. They tell you what's changeable and what's fixed. They allow you to put energy into certain directions but not into others.

In many ways, the views act as perceptual filters. To deal with the daily bombardment of data, emotions, noises, accidents, e-mail, phone calls, and other onslaughts, we channel information, we filter, we screen out the irrelevant. If we didn't, we'd go crazy.

But quite often these filters and screens blind us; they distort reality. They may cause us to stereotype, to narrow our perceptions. Especially when we are not aware of them, they lead to the automatic, the reflexive, rather than the carefully considered. Although they may lurk beneath the surface, your views are nonetheless active. And therein lies peril. "The problems with mental models lie not in whether they are right or wrong—by definition, all models are simplifications. The problems . . . arise when the models are tacit—when they exist below the level of awareness" (Senge, 1990, p. 176).

Differing Expectations of Leaders Another result of the proliferation of views on leadership is that organizations now have varying expectations of people who lead. Some organizations may still be operating in top-only mode while others will reward individuals for following the social script. Within a given organization, you may need to do some digging to understand which view or set of views predominates. Similarly, people being led now hold a wide variety of ideas about what the leader should do and be. This is especially true because of the shift in attitudes toward authority and company loyalty in recent decades.

The Personal Value of Knowing Your View A big difference we find between managers who are comfortable as leaders and those who are struggling is that the former can articulate the views and images of leadership that guide them through thick and thin and that integrate career, family, and community. Aware of their own views, these individuals are in a better position to recognize how well they match the leadership roles in their organizations and to make work and career decisions accordingly.

A Personal Vision View

To the seven views, we'd like to add one more that we call the *personal vision view* of leadership. This view assumes that how one thinks about leadership is based on one's personal vision for what he or she will accomplish in life. As a result, we assume that the individual has answered several questions about leadership in relation to his or her own life:

- Who am I?
- What do I want to become?
- How will being a leader help me in becoming who I want to be?
- How can I use my organization to fulfill this view?

This is the approach we find most useful for helping people with decision making in a proactive sense. It's also a model that will serve you well as you work through the following chapters.

Your views of leadership aren't cast in stone. At each stage along the way, you will need to question and rebuild, to embellish your concepts based on new learning. The more comprehensive your view, we suggest, the better it will guide your personal and career integration.

Look back over the views of leadership. Spend some time on the following questions:

Which view or views do you find appealing?

Which are disagreeable to you?

Have you been conscious of your own leadership views?

What views of leadership have been preferred in organizations where you have worked?

How close are the matches between your views and those of your organizations or of people you have recently led?

COSTS OF LEADERSHIP

As these views, images, and definitions of leadership have expanded, so have the expectations of leaders. As expectations have grown, so has the ambiguity of how to lead best in a particular situation. The demands by those being led are much greater, and as we noted earlier in the chapter, the context keeps changing. As a result, we see leaders becoming more vocal about the demands and costs as realities of leadership. Leaders are also questioning their own willingness to pay the costs and shoulder the burdens.

Understanding the costs is important to understanding more about the context in which you currently lead or will lead in the future. Fortunately, there is plenty of information to go on. When we interviewed managers for this book, they often stumbled over the question "Have you given conscious thought to leadership?" But they never hesitated to answer the questions about costs, sacrifices, and difficulties. Managers often spoke of "stress levels," "irritability," or "dealing with problem performers." Some bemoaned a loss of freedom. These costs were particularly painful, and our interviewees were able to articulate them quite clearly. As one interviewee said, "If you do assume the mantle, you've got to pay the price."

Here are the types of costs that our interviewees frequently mentioned. Of course, some individuals regard some of the "costs" as also rewarding in various ways.

Visibility. This is the "fishbowl" phenomenon. All eyes are on you. Who is he spending time with? Who is she including in her meetings? Why is she having lunch with X? Did you hear what he did to Y? Take a look at what she's wearing today. He's fighting with his wife again, so he's in a bad mood. One executive comments:

> Just walking out in my work area (there are ninety folks in my operation),
> I know they watch me all the time. I try to make sure that the behavior
> that they see is the behavior that I would not have a problem with if I were
> watching it in them. [But] it's like walking a tightrope. You wonder some-
> times if it's OK to let your hair down and just be yourself—or is that not
> what we typically want our leaders to be. Leaders sometimes are held to
> higher standards than others, and that can be very tough.

Public Duties. There are speeches to give and introductions to make. There are dinner parties, cocktail parties, receptions, and fund-raising activities. Visiting big-wigs need to be greeted. The more one rises in an organization, the more one takes on public relations responsibilities. These are important responsibilities, and to shirk them invites consequences.

Separation. The leader is not "one of the gang" anymore. The former peer group disappears, replaced by new peers with new toys. It's not that leaders must be iso-lated socially but rather that long-lasting, genuinely comfortable relationships often are lost and aren't easy to replace. There can be a feeling of "aloneness" in leader-ship positions.

Caretaking and Emotional Strain. Leaders need to take care of others. They play parent-referee-clergy roles that require time and energy. These roles are often not sought by leaders but imposed by their employees. There are lots of needy folks out there, and some days they all show up in your office. For many managers, re-sponsibility for direct reports weighs heavily. Said one executive:

> You have a significant measure of control over people's lives. You know, pro-
> motions and demotions and firings. You have to be willing to understand
> that and make judgments and do it extremely carefully. In a way, you're
> really fulfilling a trust that some organization is putting on you.

Stamina. Leadership requires energy, not only for oneself but also to impart to others. There are long hours, long meetings, and loss of time for family and recre-ation. There are reports, memos, and letters to be read and answered. The volume of e-mail and voice-mail messages rises exponentially with each promotion. And the travel! Those stuffy waiting rooms, bad food, cramped airline seats, and de-layed flights. Many people think leadership brings glamour and excitement, but exhaustion may be a better word.

Job Insecurity. In certain environments, leadership roles are not secure. Merit is defined and rewarded more selectively for leadership than for professional roles. Senior leaders are judged on the basis of the success of the whole enterprise, a result of many influences beyond their control. And let's be realistic: there may be someone else who really wants your leadership role or someone who just doesn't want you in it.

Less Freedom of Expression. The higher you climb in an organization, the greater the trade-offs and compromises. Anxieties come from the need to tightly control your feelings, your words. You cannot think aloud. Your comments as a senior vice president may carry far greater impact than the same comments from a department supervisor. You may want to relax, joke around, be one of the gang. But relaxation becomes a scarce commodity. You must be more conscious of your image. A show of anxiety might easily spread anxiety among your direct reports.

Infrequent Relief and Strains on Family. The leader's focus is singular. You must keep an eye on the bigger picture while also narrowing priorities. There are few breaks. You become the manager taking work home every night. While others enjoy their weekends, their parties, their vacations, you are sitting at your laptop computer, staring at spreadsheets, worrying about profit margins and labor costs. Your name is first on the "emergency call" list. This creates obvious strains on the family. As one bank executive told us:

> I think my family has probably paid more than it should. I have a tendency
> to be a workaholic, and so if anything has suffered, it's been my personal life.
> I have this psychological thing, you know—as long as it's light out, I can
> work. When the sun goes down, I go home.

Another executive experiences the problem a little differently:

> The biggest cost is actually to the self, because you're forced into limited time
> for self and family and so the self goes far down on the list. Family takes a hit,
> and you feel bad about the family. So you try to take more and more out of
> the self portion to prop up the family.

Less Supportive Feedback. When you need honest appraisal the most, you're less likely to find it. The higher one moves in an organization, the less *useful* feedback one receives. Everyone else seems to have some personal bias or agenda; information is plentiful, but the "truth" is likely to be elusive. Good leaders sometimes have "truth tellers" in their organization to help with this problem, but they are not easy to find. Here are some important questions for you to consider.

Which of these costs are you experiencing?

Which ones do you find most difficult to cope with?

What costs do you hear being expressed by others?

Which costs do you expect to grow?

What forces in your organization are driving them up?

Are any costs going down?

How might costs be lowered for you?

What strategies do you currently use to deal with the costs?

Choices in careers, choices in leadership, and choices in life bring trade-offs. There are both costs and benefits. We list the costs here because we think they are useful in understanding the realities of leadership. We don't list the rewards and benefits here, in part because they are extremely personal. Another reason that we don't list them here is that understanding the rewards and benefits will be an important part of your own journey through this book. Later chapters will touch on benefits and rewards in myriad ways. In the final chapter, we'll give you some ideas about how to weigh the costs and benefits.

SUMMARY AND SYNTHESIS

In this chapter, we have described the change in organizations from traditional hierarchies with a relatively clear definition of leadership to more complex, flattened, flexible, customer-oriented structures in which leadership is less clearly defined and possibly more costly to assume.

Look back at Figure 1.1 in Chapter One. It is intended to suggest how external realities will need to inform your personal thinking throughout this book. As you work on vision, values, and other topics, keep going back to your perceptions of the context in which you make your decisions about a leadership career.

Respond to the following questions directly in the book or in a separate journal.

1. What do you see happening "out there" in the turbulent world of organizations? Are there implications for leadership that you may not have recognized before?

_____

_____

_____

_____

_____

_____

_____

2. What forces are shaping your current feelings about being a leader? Do they pose any needs to change or opportunities for you to develop as a leader?

_____

_____

_____

_____

_____

_____

_____

Ground Your Leadership Vision in Personal Vision

This chapter explains how effective leadership depends first on one's personal vision and then one's leadership vision. By *personal vision* we mean the overarching ideal picture that you see for your life, including family, work, community life, and any other areas that you feel are important. By *leadership vision* we mean the aspect or subset of your personal vision that includes how you want to be as a leader and how your leadership will help your organization fulfill its organizational vision. In considering how you want to be as a leader, you may find that your leadership vision carries you beyond your current job or organization. Think of your leadership vision as the various roles that you might want to play as a leader, accomplishments that you'd like to achieve through leadership, and how you see your leadership work making the personal vision happen.

This chapter will lead you through a process of clarifying your personal and leadership visions. In Chapter Four, you'll explore how these visions connect to your values.

PERSONAL VISION AND ITS CONNECTION TO LEADERSHIP

In *Secrets of Effective Leadership* (1987), Fred Manske writes: "To me, a leader is a visionary who energizes others. This definition has two key dimensions: (1) creating a vision of the future and (2) inspiring people to make the vision reality" (p. 3).

We strongly agree that effectiveness in leadership begins with vision. The absence of an embracing vision quite often means a lack of direction for yourself and those for whom you may be responsible. Leadership without vision is just management, administration, or something else entirely.

We also suggest that a desire for leadership must be part of a broader personal vision. Without internal clarity about what you want for your life, your leadership will lack clear purpose, and you may find yourself leading others to a place you don't necessarily want to go. Leadership can be an instrument of personal expression that enriches your choice of trade, specialty, or vocation. Leadership can also be a vehicle a person can use to help accomplish a personal vision. If a particular leadership job or role does not foster and enhance the agendas of your personal vision, then perhaps you should either look for a leadership role that will or else say no to leadership at this time.

The Effects of a Personal Vision

Richard Castle (a fictional name) is a really bright guy. If he had become a professor, it wouldn't have surprised anyone who had known him at his Ivy League college or the large university where he earned his Ph.D. As it happened, however, he joined a large company as an "analyst." He worked his way up the line, doing larger jobs and having more people report to him. The money and promotional prospects were good, but one day he asked himself, "Why am I doing all this?"

It took a while for Rick to realize that if he didn't establish a personal reason for doing all this pyramid-climbing, he was destined to have a crisis of some kind. He needed to have a reason for working so hard, and the power, money, and glory just didn't do it for him.

When he searched his thinking, he found the answer: he could make a positive, meaningful difference in the world. He could accomplish through his work the kind of change that professors can only hope to accomplish indirectly, through their students. He could make an important part of the world more efficient and a better place for everyone.

To Rick, this seemed worthwhile. Having made that vision explicit, he could go about the tasks of learning to be the boss, doing the deals, satisfying the CEO and the corporate staff, and integrating his home and work lives.

A personal vision will have many dimensions, including ideas about your personal life, your family life, your work life, and your social life in the larger community, no matter how you choose to define the term. It may emphasize some things more than others or focus primarily on one area of your life.

To serve as a useful guide, your personal vision should do three things:

1. It should incorporate your dreams and passions; the things that excite you.

2. It should be authentic and true to your realities, anchored in who you really are. It doesn't have to meet anyone else's standards.

3. It should continue to evolve. Personal vision is not static, like a photograph, but rather like frames from a videotape that change slightly from day to day. It reflects where you are in your own evolution and where you think you are heading.

A little later in this chapter, we'll ask you to explore your personal vision systematically. But take a moment here to reflect a bit about your personal vision.

What are you passionate about?

What are your dreams?

Where do you want to be in five years? Ten years?

If you live your life to its fullest, what will you have accomplished?

What impact do you want to make?

Personal Vision and Leadership Vision

Your ability to articulate a personal vision can increase your ability to articulate a leadership vision—a picture of yourself as a leader. Your leadership vision must fit with your personal vision; it emerges from it and helps make your personal vision happen. Your leadership vision includes what you are trying to accomplish as a leader in your trade, specialty, or vocation, as well as what you might be trying to accomplish outside work.

Ordinarily, we choose a vocation—to become a doctor, carpenter, or teacher—without considering leadership as a component of that vocation. Our "career" choice, often made between the ages of eighteen and twenty-five, reflects our identity as best we understand it at that point in time. This vocational choice includes the sketch of a life plan: "to become" something, in some setting. Still to be added to the life plan is your more mature understanding of how leadership, in the context of your chosen profession, will be a vehicle for nourishing you individually and the people you are leading.

How many managers think about their leadership vision? Interviewing a technical manager with a chemical company, we asked, "Have you ever thought about a vision for yourself as a leader?" Without hesitation, he answered:

> Leadership is all about being able to formulate a vision, deciding that you want to go somewhere, that there is value in getting there, and then being able to describe that vision, to sell that vision. The word *lead* comes in [where you] really bring people with you to attain it.

We asked a facilities manager with a Navy background about his philosophy of leadership. He responded in a way that showed he'd given the question some thought: "My philosophy on leadership is that you're there to provide calm and direction. When needed, step in and help pull the wagon. For some reason, people like to follow, and they follow me fairly well."

Unfortunately, these confident answers were the exception. "Not really," was what most managers said: "I thought mainly in terms of management." "I was thinking more in terms of job and job description than I was in terms of leadership and what I had to do." "I thought one of the things I needed was the proper job title to get things done."

Your leadership vision needs to be grounded in your personal vision. Your personal vision serves your leadership vision in a very important way: it lets you know what leadership roles to accept or decline, seek or avoid. With insight into your personal vision, you'll be prepared to do intelligent negotiating. You'll have a feeling of strength and direction. You'll be able to deal with the trade-offs of your life because you'll have trust in the authenticity of your decision. Dealing with trade-offs is an important part of a leader's life.

Authenticity is key. You probably can be an "OK" manager simply by learning and practicing good techniques, but outstanding managers bring authenticity to the job. They infuse the work with their own values and experiences, are as concerned with their shortcomings as with their strengths, and never forget that they are a full human being, not just a person in a leadership role.

Over the years, leadership may become so integral to your life that you don't need to draw a clear distinction between personal vision and leadership vision. You may see no distinction between the two because you can't get where you want to go unless you're in a leadership position. Or leadership may be only a segment of your personal vision, a role that weaves in and out of your life. You are effective and feel rewarded as an individual contributor or team member, and the challenges of leadership are of no continual or consistent interest.

A Notable Example

Here's how authenticity, personal vision, and leadership vision can come together in a big way. The Estee Lauder Companies, Inc., is a $4 billion enterprise that grew from the vision and the efforts of one woman, her family, and the people she attracted to the firm. The factors that helped change young Josephine Esther Mentzer into Estee Lauder were also factors in the creation of the organization that carries her name.

Known as Esty even as a girl, Estee Lauder nurtured a personal vision from early in life. Later in life, she looked at life this way: "I want to paint a picture of the young girl I was—a girl caught up, mesmerized, by pretty things and pretty people" (Koehn, 2000, p. 17).

Several prominent personal traits are evident in Lauder's life patterns.

- She showed intense drive. Stanley Marcus of Neiman-Marcus described her as "one of the most tenacious individuals I ever met" (Arts & Entertainment Network, 1999).
- She was a competitive person and fantasized about becoming famous.
- She loved to change things, fix them up to make them prettier. Her father often admonished her not to "fiddle with other people's faces" when she would try to improve how adults looked. Her daughter-in-law discovered that Estee was forever rearranging the furniture in her son's home.
- She was good at selling from an early age.

Fortunately, she had certain opportunities and role models—an uncle who made skin cream, female relatives who ran a department store in Queens, the cosmetics pioneers Elizabeth Arden and Helena Rubenstein. She also encountered new social conditions—the emergence of women in the social and working worlds of the mid-twentieth century—and made the most of them.

She had a vision, was aware of a good part of it, and lived it. She invented herself, liked what she saw, and kept on inventing. But how does her story differ from that of many a saleswoman, designer, or portrait artist—the story of any of several kinds of individual contributors? She also had a leadership vision.

"I wanted to be at the top of something," Lauder wrote, looking back on her life (Arts & Entertainment Network, 1999). And she found that she was effective at gathering others to help her and at directing their efforts. Thus her personal vision extended to and included a vision of herself as a leader of an organization. It specified that she would be an active, driving leader.

Knowing a bit about the passions and interests of this woman, you won't be surprised that her motto—her vision for the organization—was "There are no homely women, only careless ones." She took her own view of the world and made it the mission of the company. Her vision became the basis for its vision.

EXERCISES TO CLARIFY YOUR PERSONAL VISION

Before we look further at leadership vision, let's focus on your personal vision. Counselors and trainers of managers know that great clarity of personal purpose may be hiding just under the surface and that a bit of coaxing may be all that's needed to reveal it.

As a child, you may have had no problem "knowing" that you would someday become an astronaut, a professional athlete, a teacher, or a doctor. As you grew into your teens and then into your college years, you may have expressed what you then "knew" about yourself by seeking out other young people who shared your interests in learning, sports, partying, politics, or volunteering. Later you began to see yourself in adult roles as family and community member, and as a participant in formal work organizations. Leadership visions were perhaps woven into your life at various stages. These images and scripts may not have been spelled out or written on notes you taped to the wall, but they were and still are there. We're asking you to coax them back out.

A few people really have no internal map, no polestar, no foundational sense on which to design and build a future self. Some people are not particularly thoughtful about their lives and rarely think proactively about them. But since you're reading this book, you're unlikely to be one of them.

Having your sense of purpose or vision available for discussion can be extremely helpful. It can't be as useful if it stays below the level of awareness. An inarticulate vision leaves too much to chance. It prevents its owner from being proactive, leaving only a passive, opportunistic approach to career and life. Things might work out very, very well—or they might not, even though they could have.

It's better to clarify and discover your personal vision. We say "discover" because a vision is not created from scratch, not adopted, grafted, or otherwise artificially induced. Clarifying your vision is a sort of journey, but it's not a shopping trip.

Yet it is a process of looking in the likely places for the important elements of that vision and putting pieces together to form a conscious, meaningful, and integrated picture. You discover your vision by looking at yourself honestly. Sometimes that's a struggle. A few introspective exercises can be helpful. Your personal vision may not come out crystal-clear, but it should be more visible than it was.

Figure 3.1 lists some methods that we'll explore. None is an automatic winner, but most people benefit from looking at themselves in one or more of the indicated ways.

Tell Your Own Story

If we wish to know about a man we ask, "What is his story—his real, inmost story?" For each of us is a biography, . . . a singular narrative which is constructed continually, unconsciously, by, through, and in us—through our perceptions, our feelings, our thoughts, our notions. Biologically, physiologically, we are not so different from each other; historically, as narratives, we are each of us unique [Sacks, 1970, pp. 110–111].

There's a novel in you, though it may not be fiction: the one you're writing about your own life. Narrative is innate to human growth, and personal vision

---

Figure 3.1 Ways to Clarify Your Personal Vision

- Tell Your Own Story
- Reflect on Your Daydreams
- Look for Patterns in Events, Behaviors, Focus, and Energy
- Take Lessons from Role Models
- Assess How You Feel About Power
- Assess Your Responses to Conflict
- Note Your Creative Involvement
- Follow Your Intuition

---

often springs from myth or one's imagination. When people discover, create, invent, build businesses, have families, compose symphonies, or fly to the moon, they do it to fulfill a story that they've been telling themselves and others.

For many of us, important early leadership stories find their setting in sports. One team-conscious retail chain executive told us:

> When I was ten years old, I guess I was timid at the plate. I remember [a coach] putting his arm around me and saying that if I don't swing, I'll never hit the ball. That kind of reassured me.
>
> I got interested in leadership in high school, when I was exposed to team competitions and sports. What interested me about it was the coaches who came in touch with me . . . and seeing what a person can do with a group of people who are motivated.
>
> I've always seen that if I can do the best that I can do, that's all that's really required. In a team concept of leadership, if we can get people to do the best they can do, that's really success.

Perhaps we shouldn't be surprised that with this grounding of leadership style in his early years, this man says leadership keeps him "young in mind."

The richer and more compelling you can make the story of yourself, the stronger your creations will be. People tell and retell their stories until they get them right. Your own story is connected to stories you inherited from others. We are not isolated creatures. This story from one of our interviewees gives a sense of that continuity:

> I had an older brother that I really looked up to, nine years older than me. I was in about fourth grade when he got killed in Vietnam. At that time, my mother told me that I had to be the head of the household. I think that had a profound effect on me. That was a catalyst. I went from being a child to being responsible from that day forward.
>
> I've been in leadership types of positions ever since I was in high school. In high school, it started out with sports. Then I got real serious about politics in high school, and I got involved in some political groups in the sixties. [Now] I'm involved in a number of different nonprofit organizations . . . , and I have leadership roles in every one of them.

Some stories, like splitting the atom, conquering flight, or curing diseases, may take generations to tell and complete. People whose stories are picked up and used by other folks may be called pioneers or leaders.

At an early age, we begin to see our lives as stories. During adolescence, we realize that we can be the authors of that story. Accepting responsibility for being the author of one's own life doesn't come easily to some people. Others relish being able to rewrite themselves from time to time.

As the years pass, we revise and improvise further, but the basic theme of our stories generally shows great continuity over time. Perhaps a teacher's theme is *helping others achieve potential,* whether those others are students, family, or friends. The news reporter's theme may be *articulating the community for the community* so that people may better comprehend their environment. The doctor, the nurse, the neurophysiologist may express continuity in a theme of *healing* or finding causes and cures of disease. The engineer's theme might be *invention;* the lawyer's, *justice.*

Our stories and themes inform our visions, including our visions of leadership. Within the larger story of your life, then, your view of yourself as a leader emerges.

Take a moment to think about your story and its recurring themes.

If you wrote the story of your life as a series of headlines, what would they be?

What events in your life have inspired your passion?

What events have held the most learning for you?

Where have your main ideas come from?

What are some major themes of your story?

How actively have you written the story of your own life?

How well is it hanging together?

Do you like where it's taking you?

Is leadership a part of the story?

Reflect on Your Daydreams

In quiet moments throughout the day, you "space out" into imaginings and better worlds. Perhaps it is when you're alone, heading to or from work, or maybe while walking the dog. Perhaps it's during one of "those" meetings.

Daydreams are important. They are telling you something. They are connecting your real present to a possible future. They contain your hopes about how you will turn out as a person and some sketchy plans for how to do it. Daydreams are telling you important things about your vision by revealing images of yourself—the kinds of successes you're having, how you see yourself as a winner or hero, the kinds of situations you're in, and what you do to make things come out well.

One consummate dreamer, Thomas Jefferson, imagined a set of principles about how free people should live in relationship to their government and then reflected those views in a lifetime spent founding and expanding a vast country, creating a university, and securing such documents as the Bill of Rights.

Dr. Martin Luther King Jr. said, "I have a dream," to a crowd in front of the Lincoln Memorial in 1963. His words and deeds helped crystallize a nonviolent civil rights movement.

Steve Case had "a boyhood dream of building a company that shaped public consciousness," according to the founder and chairman emeritus of America Online, James Kimsey (Leibovich, 1998, p. 3). Case began to fulfill that dream in his early twenties when he joined AOL in 1983, when it wasn't much more than a start-up. Today he is chairman and CEO of AOL Time Warner, the world's leading interactive services company. The desire to be the leader of an organization that shapes the way the world thinks and acts has been his personal vision and his leadership vision. Says Paul Noglows, a technology industry analyst at San Francisco–based Hambrecht & Quist, "When our children read about the history of the Internet, they're going to be reading about Steve Case" (p. 19).

Not all dreams are as broad and inspiring as these are. Dreams of smaller scope can be equally inspiring. And they don't have to be entirely original. Dr. King borrowed from Gandhi; Jefferson borrowed from the philosophers of the European Enlightenment. Steve Case didn't found AOL; he just put heart, soul, and his own dreams behind it. But ultimately, the dream does have to be 100 percent yours as well.

As the song in the Broadway musical *Finian's Rainbow* put it, people will "follow the fellow who follows the dream."

Take a moment to jot down what you've been daydreaming about lately, and remind yourself for the next few days to jot down what you see in your daydreams. Apply what you see to the following questions.

> Into what kind of future do you project yourself?
>
> What daydreams attract you the most?
>
> Who's with you in your daydreams?
>
> What kind of person are you becoming in your daydreams? What are you doing?
>
> What are you accomplishing in your daydreams?
>
> What impact do you have?
>
> Do your daydreams include glimpses of leadership?

Look for Patterns in Events, Behaviors, Focus, and Energy

Another way to bring your vision to light is to look for *patterns*. We're not suggesting anything really complex here, but when you "play back the tape" of your recent life, don't you see some patterns? Patterns will certainly be there, although not always neatly labeled. They may be more obvious to people around you than they are to you.

Let's start with the broader patterns—the "macro" view. Look at the important events during the past year or two—especially key projects, events, and relationships at work. When do you tend to have success and when not? When have you been happiest and when not? Which situations do you find easy or hard? For what kinds of things are you asked to join in? Which of these really interest you?

A number of factors could be making certain activities successful, enjoyable, easy, and attractive for you. What's the underlying theme in these situations? What do they have in common that produces the positive experience? It is common for these outcomes to be closely related to how we see ourselves and therefore also how we want to be seen. You can call this "self-image." Noticing when and where you feel a positive self-image is also a way to identify the vision you are trying to project—a picture of where you're trying to go in life.

At closer range among your behaviors are the roles you play when you're in groups. There are two kinds of learning available here: one has to do with how eagerly you engage directly in leadership roles and what kind of leadership roles you embrace; the other has to do with where you typically try to lead the groups you are in, from whatever roles you play.

Which roles do you typically play in group situations? The organizer? The formal leader? The joker? The analyst? The peacemaker or mediator? The salesman? The summarizer? The advocate for the underdog? Some roles are more visibly "the leader" than others, but they can all contribute to the overall leadership effort.

Where have you tried to take the group? Do you try to make something new and different happen? Do you try to improve on existing systems? Do you try to make a short-term "win" for yourself, the organization, or both? Do you think more about developing the members of the group and the group as a whole? Do you think more about the bottom line, shareholders, and customers? When you have the opportunity to be a formal leader, what do you do with it? To the extent that your behavior in a group reflects something important about who you are, what is that "something"?

Now let's move in even closer, to a relatively micro view. The world is full of things to do, see, be part of, make happen. Each of us makes choices about where to concentrate our efforts and what to ignore as background. Where you choose to focus can indicate something about what is central to your vision.

Remember the story about the three scientists walking along the beach? The biologist, geologist, and astronomer were at the same place, doing the same thing, but saw rather different things. Consider these observations, which could be made by different people attending the same meeting:

"Look at all the wasted effort—talk, talk, talk and no outcome. Why doesn't the boss just decide? This is no way to run an organization."

"Isn't it great that everyone can participate! When I'm the boss, I'm going to do things in this way too."

"Why is everyone talking about new products and new selling approaches, and not one word about profits?"

"Same old, same old. Not a creative thought in the room. Sam had an idea, but no one listened. This meeting could have been held three years ago."

"It's important to have better products. High-quality products sell themselves, eventually."

"The boss is doing a great job of pulling the group together—getting everyone behind her so she can present a unified front. Good job!"

"I need to do something to help the boss. In fact, I know what I want to say. . . ."

"I don't care about the 'new' products, which I don't think are so new. Nothing will work unless you know how to sell it!"

People look at life in different ways. For people you know well, you can usually anticipate their responses to a particular situation. They can probably anticipate your responses as well. Such predictability provides important information on a person's vision and leadership style.

Finally, where do you invest your *energies* when you really do have a choice? What situations, events, and activities attract you? Look at your voluntary and discretionary activities, and check for patterns in what you find important. As you do so, recognize that you are probably exercising a degree of choice even in situations that feel like obligations. We each have our ways of drifting into the chores, errands, and commitments that we prefer!

Try consulting a few people whose opinions you trust as you ask the following questions.

When are you happiest or most successful? When least?

When do you feel most focused?

What captures your attention?

What situations energize you?

What kinds of situations get you to drop everything else?

Do you become focused with other people?

Does leadership energize or drain you?

What roles do you play in groups?

What feedback have you received about your roles with other people?

What other patterns do you see?

Take Lessons from Role Models

To ask people about their role models is to ask them about their own aspirations. A person who names Bill Gates as a role model has a very different vision than one who names Nelson Mandela, Katie Couric, or "my Aunt Charlene."

Role models can be real or fictional, famous or personal. What's important is that you have been thinking about that person's image and found something attractive in it. It is that "something attractive" that we want to capture.

It isn't enough just to pick a hero. You need to expand your thoughts by asking why that person attracts you. Do you name Bill Gates because he is bright, because he's the richest person in the world, or because he built an enormously successful company? Do you choose Nelson Mandela because he overcame adversity, because he became a national savior, or because of the way he performed in office? Is Katie Couric your role model because she has secured and retained her position on the *Today* show when most women are removed from the media once their "perceived youth" starts to wane? Or did you choose her for her strength in overcoming the hardship of her spouse's death and her decision to become a spokeswoman against a dreaded disease? What do you admire about Aunt Charlene? Perhaps the fact that she built a successful retail operation in California, travels all over the world, and doesn't have to ask anyone's permission to do anything!

Here is how one interviewee articulated what he learned from one of several role models in his career:

> I had one boss who was actually the CFO at *Esquire* magazine. His philosophy [was contained in the statement] that he would never let anybody go unless he was satisfied that he had done everything that he could to make that person work out in the position. In that statement he was essentially telling me that I needed to take as much responsibility as the other person and do everything that I could to make a situation work. That's a large, transcending statement. People look for the easy way out, but there has to be a lot of personal ownership in leadership.

Spend some time thinking about your own role models. Make a short list of candidates.

Who are your role models?

Why are they role models for you?

Are their personal characteristics similar to yours, or do you admire these people because they are so different from you?

In what ways have your role models exhibited leadership?

Assess How You Feel About Power

How do you feel about having and using power? We're talking here about the power to make things happen, to get things done by "working the system." Power is a factor in many people's personal vision, although they may not label it "power." The word *power* has many negative connotations. Most people are more comfortable with words like *influence, impact,* or *effectiveness.* But power is a part of leadership. If leadership is a part of your personal vision, then power is likely embedded somewhere in there too.

One definition of power is the ability or capacity to act or perform effectively. Isn't that what leadership is about? One executive whom we interviewed reflected this spirit to a striking degree:

> I would like to be seen as an individual to whom organizations turn in order to basically rescue the people in the organization. In companies with people in danger—in whatever corporations I've worked for—I want to be known as the guy who turned the business around and made it successful and all the people in it happy. I would like to be known as someone who developed good people, . . . a developer of talent. I'd like to look at an organization and say, "He's mine, she's mine, she's mine, he's mine."

Other people cannot take on a power role without a great deal of gnashing of teeth. It never was in their life plan to take power, so when the opportunities arise, as they do in any leadership position, old scripts about the importance of modesty, fairness, not stepping on toes, and so forth may stand in the way of their taking control. This sort of interference isn't easy to sort out, but it can be worth your time to try.

Give some thought to some questions like these.

Do you enjoy power?

When and where do you feel powerful?

Do you admire others who exhibit power?

What do you do with your power? Does it work?

How do you feel and act when you don't have a feeling of power?

What old scripts about power may be interfering with your exercise of leadership?

Assess Your Responses to Conflict

Conflict can be informative. It can indicate what you hold valuable and are willing to defend and protect. Whether you are right or wrong in any particular situation is not what's important here. Neither are we concerned with how well you fought for your position or whether you won. What we do care about is what you engaged in conflict *about*.

Some people really don't have any important conflicts. Perhaps they feel they never win or it takes too much out of them or it creates permanent enemies or it doesn't belong in polite society. If one of these is true for you, then you'll need to think in terms of "what I would have liked to fight for" instead of what you did fight for. The data may not be as clear but still might prove useful.

We assume that you agree that it is worthwhile to have productive conflicts in organizations and therefore that you have some to review in your mind. If you don't already know this, and you're not quite willing to take it on faith, we refer you to Sessa, 1994, who shows how conflict can be good, especially in teams and especially when team members resolve to learn from the conflict rather than just react negatively to it. There's nothing like a conflict to focus an issue.

Open, major confrontations may be easiest for you to consider, but minor conflicts are also informative. In certain situations, you may simply have said that enough was enough, insisted that something be done a new way, or strongly resisted a change. At the most visible level, you may have declined or lost a leadership role rather than do things in what you felt was a "wrong" way—in the spirit of "I'd rather be right than president." Perhaps you changed jobs so you could have things your way. Also consider less visible situations, such as these:

- You helped create an alliance to win against an opposing alliance.

- You found yourself in a prolonged debate about the merits of something— lots of memos, e-mails, meetings, and so forth.

- You told someone in a senior position that doing it your way wasn't just better but a *lot* better or maybe even the only way to succeed.

- You have been accused of being boringly repetitive about a certain cause.

- A particular issue is so important that folks who don't agree with you are never part of your network.

- Your friends know not to discuss certain things with you because they know the strong reaction it will trigger.

What is your personal response to conflict?

> What ideas or goals have you fought for in recent years?
>
> What have you "gone to the mat" about?
>
> What tends to be at stake when you find yourself in conflict with others?
>
> What do some past experiences of conflict suggest about your personal vision and yourself as a leader?

Note Your Creative Involvement

Creativity is a heightened form of focus and energy, a condition of deep involvement with whatever you're doing. It doesn't happen by chance or without expenditure of desire and effort. People who spend their lives being creative will freely admit that it takes preparation and hard work. But the benefits are tremendous.

As Julia Cameron writes in *The Artist's Way* (1992), "Many of us find that we have squandered our own creative energies by investing proportionately in the lives, hopes, dreams and plans of others." If we search for that inner core of creativity, we "will become more able to articulate our own boundaries, dreams and authentic goals" (p. 6). Cameron's work is about helping others unleash their creativity.

If you have an area of life in which you try to be creative, it's worth exploring what it says about your personal vision. Don't skip past it just because it doesn't seem to be related to what you get paid for. It may tell you more about your passion, desires, and energy.

> When do you feel most creative?
>
> When do you feel loose and flowing?
>
> Do these feelings result from being creative in your job?
>
> Do you think of leadership as creative? How so? How not?
>
> Does your organization encourage your creativity?
>
> How do you use your creativity outside your job or leadership role?

Follow Your Intuition

Some of us rely a good deal on intuition and use it to help make decisions. Intuition is a way of knowing, of understanding the world. It's a way to see how things come together, where they came from, how they are connected, and where they are likely to go. It is a kind of pattern identification, without having all the hard data to support conclusions. It's a feeling that says, "I don't trust myself about everything, but on this topic I seem to know what's right. When it comes to this subject, I win by following my feelings."

There's a connection between intuition and personal vision. Both are based on parts of ourselves that aren't fully conscious. Both have things to say about what makes sense and what feels right. Both can lead us to where we belong.

If there are areas in which you have found your intuition to be particularly valuable, those areas are likely to feature in your personal vision. Some people have this trust in their intuition when it comes to selecting employees. For others, it has to do with which products will sell or how fast to expand a business. Intuition tells certain other people when it is time to focus on other arenas besides work.

Especially relevant for readers of this book is this sequence of questions: What does my intuition tell me about the connection between me and leadership? Do I have something important to accomplish through an organization? Will people follow my lead? Am I ready to handle the challenge now? Is this the time and place? What else could I be doing? Ask yourself these questions and the ones below.

Do you value your intuition?

Do you trust it?

What has happened when you have acted on intuition?

In what situations has it seemed most reliable and perceptive?

Does your intuition work well about people?

Has it played a role in your leadership work to date?

What does your intuition tell you about whether you should be a leader?

A Synthesis

Look back over your responses to the questions in this chapter. Begin to synthesize from the sets that were most productive for you:

- Where is your life story heading?

- What better world do you like to imagine?

- Who inspires you?

- How do you see yourself in relation to power and conflict?

- What gives you energy?

- What makes you feel most creative and intuitive?

- What makes you happiest?

1. Elaborate on your responses in thought and writing, either here or in a separate journal. Do your thoughts point in consistent directions?

_____

_____

_____

_____

_____

2. Without analyzing too much where you are right now, write some statements that begin to capture a sense of your personal vision or future picture. Think about where you'd like to go regarding your work, family, community, and any other aspect of life that matters to you. Think about the themes you want to see present in your life. Think about what you want to accomplish in life. What governs your life? What are your desires and passions? What is your story? How might you refocus your energy around that story, that vision? Don't worry about clear sentences or correct grammar. Just capture some phrases.

_____

_____

_____

_____

_____

As your current personal vision becomes clearer, you may have to ask yourself some hard questions about it. Are you being truly honest? Is this what you want or what others want for you? Are the elements of your vision compatible, or are there contradictions? What will be the obstacles in reaching this future state?

As we suggested earlier, a personal vision evolves. New events, additional ideas, and different ways of thinking will cause your vision to shift over time. It is important to think about how these influences affect where you are and where you are heading. At times of important transition in your life, you may wish to redo this kind of exercise.

What actually happens once you have a clearer personal vision?

- You'll be clearer about your intended direction in life—where you want to go, why, and what you'll do when you get there.

- You'll know what you'd like to test or learn as you navigate any organization's opportunities. You will be better able to make decisions about the paths and options presented to you.

- You'll know your passions and priorities. You'll know what you can trade off and what you should not compromise.

- You'll be better able to move toward roles that will let you express what you have to offer, as a leader or in other roles.

- You'll have a sense of the decision process—how it happens that some people find their way to leadership roles and others elect not to.

YOUR LEADERSHIP VISION

At the start of this chapter, we defined leadership vision as an ideal picture of what you might do as a leader and how this role should fit within your broader personal vision. Having a clear leadership vision allows you to make better decisions about the leadership roles you pursue. It sets an agenda for what to do next in your leadership life. Your leadership vision can also help you recognize the responsible choice in a given situation. It will help answer questions such as "Why am I doing what I'm doing?" and "Do I accept the trade-offs I'm making in order to succeed as a leader?" A leadership vision also lends a confident, steady sense of identity amid chaos.

A key task of leadership is providing an organizational vision. An organizational vision implies people coming together to pursue a common future goal. It is the leadership that helps define the activities, outcomes, and measurements toward that end. When there is significant congruence, one's leadership vision will be the means by which one's personal vision and one's organizational vision are accomplished.

Now begin to craft a leadership vision either here or in your journal.

1. How much of a leader have you already been in your life and career?

_____

_____

_____

_____

2. What attracts you to leadership? What aspects of it are not appealing?

_____

_____

_____

_____

3. Is your leadership role helping you realize your personal vision? If a headline appeared about you as a leader, what would you want it to say?

_____

_____

_____

_____

4. What or whom do you need to lead in order to achieve your vision? If you are already an experienced leader, do you need to start a new organization or apply your talents to some new arena or career?

_____

_____

_____

_____

_____

5. What degree of commitment to leadership is compatible with your overall personal vision?

_____

_____

_____

_____

_____

6. Does your current position develop your leadership? What new leadership opportunity might make you drop everything else?

_____

_____

_____

_____

_____

7. What else do you need to know before you can be clear about your leadership vision? For example, do you need to know more about your abilities, your way of making an impact, how you contribute to others, personal benefits and rewards, or how you can help others make sense of the world?

_____

_____

_____

_____

_____

_____

8. Are you thinking about putting your leadership vision on hold until later in your career? Why?

_____

_____

_____

_____

_____

_____

SUMMARY AND SYNTHESIS

In the novel *The Unbearable Lightness of Being,* Milan Kundera (1984) suggests that for everyone there is an "Es muss sein!"—an "It must be!" or overriding necessity that governs the person's life. Insofar as it's possible to divide people into categories, the surest criterion is the deep-seated desires that orient them to one or another lifelong activity.

We've been asking you specific questions at points throughout this chapter. Now we'd like to ask you to begin writing your personal vision.

1. How would you take all of the responses you have been making to the various questions and begin writing what your personal vision really is? How specific can you be? How will it be a guiding force?

_____

_____

_____

_____

_____

2. Look back at this personal vision. Is there a place for leadership in it? Do you have a clear sense of a leadership vision from your responses to the earlier questions? What is that leadership vision? Try to capture it here.

_____

_____

_____

_____

_____

3. Do you see any conflicts between your personal vision, your leadership vision, and your current position or organization?

_____

_____

_____

_____

_____

It's OK if you can't answer these questions definitively at this point. That is what the rest of this book is about. The final chapter will bring you back to this level of questions and ask you to be more specific about your personal and leadership visions. Now it is time to fill in gaps by looking at your values, your abilities, and the other arenas of your life.

Base Your Leadership Values on Personal Values

Values are standards or principles that guide your actions and beliefs. They define what is good and worthwhile for you. Much has been said and written about values in relation to leadership. This chapter argues that being aware of your personal values strengthens you as a leader and helps you get the most personal reward from your leadership work.

The chapter includes exercises for uncovering your core values and seeing how they interrelate. It also discusses values conflicts, as well as connections between your values and leadership choices.

VISION, VALUES, AND BEHAVIOR

The markers of your values are, of course, your behaviors. They reveal the principles by which you are actually living. At some level, you are deciding, consciously or not, how to use your energy. This line of thinking implies the need for a close connection between values and personal vision. It implies the importance of recognizing the congruence or incongruence between your personal vision and your values and behaviors.

In concert with your personal and leadership visions, your values should drive your major decisions. The familiar admonition to "walk your talk" means reflecting your values in your actions. For example, many executives we have talked with have made a commitment to not work on the weekends because of a desire to spend time with their family. Their action is driven by the value they place on family time. Are there times when people who hold this value have to make an exception?

Yes, but they don't lose sight of the basic value, and they continue to act on it most of the time.

We are often unconscious of the values that shape our acts. At times, we operate from socially imposed values that may not be conscious or important to us personally, such as the blind pursuit of financial success. At other times, we operate from personally held values that also lie beneath the surface of our thoughts, such as a sense of continual responsibility for others.

Why We Need to Be Clear About Values

Warren Wilhelm, vice president for corporate education at Allied Signal, agrees that values were, are, and always will be of primary importance in our lives as humans and our lives as leaders. But Wilhelm also says that increasingly, effective leaders will be those who are aware of and act on their values:

> Leadership without direction is useless. Uninformed by ideas about what is good and bad, right and wrong, worthy and unworthy, it is not only inconsistent but dangerous. As the pace of change in our world continues to accelerate, strong basic values become increasingly necessary to guide leadership behavior [Wilhelm, 1996, pp. 222–223].

The reasoning about values here parallels the reasoning about vision in Chapter Three. When your values are clear and conscious, they provide the foundation for developing the skills, confidence, and competencies that are needed in leadership roles. Many people try to do this in reverse order. That is, they determine their skills and competencies and then try to recast them as values they really want to live by. But short of spiritual conversion, values are too central and too integral to your makeup to be changed for pragmatic reasons.

Conscious clarity of values is an asset. Maybe life will be kind to you and place you only in situations that call for rational, objective decisions and give you lots of time to prepare for them. But more likely, in leadership roles, you may need, without much warning, to make decisions that go beyond objective judgments and require clarity of values. Chances are good that you'll be dropped into at least one hot-spot job, with no easy answers and little time to prepare. Your first decisions may test your clarity of values more than your brains, training, network of relationships, or anything else about you.

The importance of having clear values in such situations is that it conveys clarity of purpose, not only about yourself as a decision-maker but also about the mission of the organization. Having clear values and awareness of their priority in your life will be important also when conflicts arise in operational settings; resolving these conflicts will be easier if the values underlying them have already been sorted out.

Some organizations are held together not so much by operating systems as by a common belief in certain important values. This type of situation may become quite common as the century advances. The management of loosely held but interlocking systems is a primary and growing challenge for today's top executives.

It may seem possible for an organization to be a purely pragmatic, mercantile venture—"our only value is making money." But we have yet to encounter that organization. There are always additional values operating in the minds and behaviors of the key players.

Are There Right and Wrong Values for Leaders?

It is tempting to try to name appropriate and inappropriate values for good leadership. Isn't it better to be fair, loyal, honest? Can anyone who is manipulative, autocratic, narcissistic, greedy, or selfish be an effective leader? We'd like to say no, but we've seen situations in which people with these traits are nevertheless considered reasonably good leaders.

Whether or not there are right or wrong values for leaders to hold, the alignment of who you are with what you're trying to do may be more important than whether you hold one particular value or another. What matters most is that you know your own values and know that they match your vision.

Ben Cohen and Jerry Greenfield shared a common dream ever since their high school days in the 1960s on Long Island. What was it? Ice cream.

"They were the two slowest, fattest kids in the gym class," notes their Web page on the history of Ben & Jerry's Homemade, Inc. Two other leading values of the two were friendship and the hopes of the sixties. Nearly forty years after they met, ice cream, friendship, and sixties-consciousness were still at the heart of their amazing success. The story of their start-up and success is well documented— $12,000 in cash, a $5 correspondence course in ice-cream making, a renovated gas station, . . . They had a good idea, got good press coverage, expanded wisely, and found themselves in charge of a company much larger than they ever imagined they'd be running.

Other values high on their list and reflected actively in their leadership are the following:

Creativity—there's often a better way; there's no need to just live with tradition.

Equality—everyone likes to feel important; hierarchy subtracts from good relationships.

Social responsibility—successful people must "give back" to their workers and the community.

Quality—only the best will do!

Fun—it's not worth doing if it isn't fun to do.

You can find the full story of how the values drove the business in their book *Ben and Jerry's Double Dip: Lead with Your Values and Make Money, Too* (Cohen and Greenfield, 1997).

UNDERSTANDING YOUR CORE VALUES

Not all values share equal rank or importance. The phrase "core values" refers to the most important ones in your personal system of values. Your core values drive your life decisions and your decisions about when you want to lead, how you want to lead, and how much you want to lead. Becoming aware of them is job number one, because once established, they will strongly influence what you pay attention to, how you make choices, and what you will defend in a conflict.

You may think that you already know your core values, but without having done any formal work on them, it's unlikely that you do. Articulating your operative core values can be extremely difficult. Even under the best conditions, the task requires some honest, lengthy reflective time and probably needs to be done several times before you have captured them accurately.

It isn't easy to clarify core values. There are forces working against you. Most of us like to repeat politically and socially acceptable statements to some degree. Most of us don't see ourselves very accurately. We like to lie to ourselves sometimes. Also, how we operationalize our core values may change gradually over time. Sometimes a core value isn't recognized, even though it led to some truly valued outcome or accomplishment, and so the value gets left off the list. Elucidation isn't simple, but it can be done.

What are some of the core values that we see driving people's lives at home and at work? For businesspeople, some core values may relate mainly to accomplishments:

Power, control, ambition

Financial independence or success

Helping people who deserve help

Being a responsible person in family and community

Working toward professional excellence

Working toward entrepreneurial success

Other core values may have more to do with interpersonal relationships, within the organization (with peers, superiors, and direct reports) and outside as well (with clients, stakeholders, and customers):

Honesty and integrity in dealings with others

Upholding the mission of the organization

Respect for other people's needs and uniqueness

Respect for the value of group decisions

The following set of exercises will help you to identify your core values and evaluate them in terms of priority, congruence with your actual behavior, and compatibility or conflict between opposing values. Keep in mind that some values change over time. What is important to a person at age thirty is very different from what is important to that person at age fifty-five.

Defining Your Values

Use Figure 4.1 (or a photocopy of it) to rate how important each general value is to you. Add any other general values that we may have overlooked. Do this now before continuing with the text.

Figure 4.1 How Often Do You Value These Things?

Rate each value on this list according to its importance to you. Write the value below the heading you deem most appropriate. Add to your lists any other values you prize.

Achievement—a sense of accomplishment, mastery, goal achievement

Activity—fast-paced, highly active work

Advancement—growth, seniority, and promotion resulting from work well done

Adventure—new and challenging opportunities, excitement, risk

Aesthetics—appreciation of beauty in things, ideas, surroundings, personal space

Affiliation—interaction with other people, recognition as a member of a particular group, involvement, belonging

Affluence—high income, financial success, prosperity

Authority—position and power to control events and other people's activities

Autonomy—ability to act independently with few constraints, self-sufficiency, self-reliance, ability to make most decisions and choices

Balance—lifestyle that allows for a balance of time for self, family, work, and community

Challenge—continually facing complex and demanding tasks and problems

Change and variation—absence of routine; work responsibilities, daily activities, or settings that change frequently; unpredictability

Collaboration—close, cooperative working relationships with groups

Community—serving and supporting a purpose that supersedes personal desires, "making a difference"

Competency—demonstrating high proficiency and knowledge, showing above-average effectiveness and efficiency at tasks

Competition—rivalry with winning as the goal

Courage—willingness to stand up for one's beliefs

Creativity—discovering, developing, or designing new ideas, formats, programs, or things; demonstrating innovation and imagination

Diverse perspectives—unusual ideas and opinions, points of view that may not seem right or be popular at first but bear fruit in the long run

Duty—respect for authority, rules, and regulations

Economic security—steady and secure employment, adequate financial reward, low risk

Enjoyment—fun, joy, and laughter

Fame—prominence, being well known

Family—spending time with partner, children, parents, or extended family

Friendship—close personal relationships with others

Health—physical and mental well-being, vitality

Helping others—helping people attain their goals, providing care and support

Humor—the ability to laugh at oneself and life

Influence—having an impact or effect on the attitudes or opinions of other people, persuasiveness

Inner harmony—happiness, contentment, being at peace with oneself

Integrity—acting in accordance with moral and ethical standards; honesty, sincerity, truth; trustworthiness

Figure 4.1 How Often Do You Value These Things? Cont'd.

Justice—fairness, equality, "doing the right thing"
Knowledge—the pursuit of understanding, skill, and expertise; continuous learning
Location—choice of a place to live that is conducive to one's lifestyle
Love—involvement in close, affectionate relationships; intimacy
Loyalty—faithfulness; dedication to individuals, traditions, or organizations
Order—stability, routine, predictability, clear lines of authority, standardized procedures
Personal development—dedication to maximizing one's potential
Physical fitness—staying in shape through exercise and physical activity
Recognition—positive feedback and public credit for work well done; respect and admiration
Responsibility—dependability, reliability, accountability for results
Self-respect—pride, self-esteem, sense of personal identity
Spirituality—strong spiritual or religious beliefs, moral fulfillment
Status—being respected for one's job or one's association with a prestigious group or organization
Wisdom—sound judgment based on knowledge, experience, and understanding

Always	Often	Sometimes	Seldom	Never

If you are like most executives, most of your values fell into the first two categories, always valued and often valued. You recognized many of the values as worthwhile concepts and therefore avoided rating them as seldom or never valued. Unfortunately, you can't really value so many things with equally high frequency. If you tried to do so, you wouldn't be able to keep up with all that you're trying to do.

Reexamine the items on your always valued list.

- Is it possible that some of these values were more important to you in the past but you continue to cling to them?

- Have you included some of the values because to do so would be politically or socially correct? Do these values really have meaning for you?

- Have you rated a value highly because someone else might have done so?

See what values you can reassign from always valued to a more accurate category.

After cleaning house in this way, you may have eight or ten values identified as always valued. A dozen should be your upper limit. Now look at the items you said you valued often. If that list has become crowded, clean house there too by asking questions like the ones you asked before. For example:

- How did you determine that this value fit under often valued rather than sometimes valued?

- Would other people say you hold this value?

Core values are the core of who you are as a person. They are the values for which you would likely fight, quit a job, or leave a relationship. They are the values that appear in the always valued column.

Making these choices isn't easy. Continue to experiment, moving the values among the columns until you believe that their arrangement represents you accurately.

Determining Congruence

Congruence refers to the match between your values and your words and actions. You actually hold values in three different ways: you have values that you hold internally, values that you state in speech, and values that are reflected in your actions. Do your speech and other signals convey the values in your head? Do your actions conform with your thoughts and speech?

We often find a disparity between what we say (our stated values) and what we do (our active values). Although you may not be able to erase the gaps and conflicts in your values, it's important to know where they are.

It's not easy to see the values playing out in your own behavior. For the following exercise, you will probably need some help from friends who know you well. Also, it can be quite difficult to acknowledge incongruities and gaps. We're generally not proud of them. But be tough!

Matching Values with Action This exercise is a check on your words; it asks you to support your position. In the previous exercise, you identified things that you always, often, or sometimes value. Now go over those items and list the actions that you think demonstrate how you live out each value. If you said that you always value courage or risk taking, where has this shown up in your actions? If you say you always value diverse perspectives, how often have you made sure that really different viewpoints have been thoroughly heard? If you say you always value creativity, when did you last cause a stir with a new idea?

Which of your highly rated values are most clearly endorsed by your actions? Perhaps some values should be demoted on your list because your actions don't indicate strong support.

Now look back at the section in Chapter Three that dealt with seeking patterns (page 41). Did that section generate any evidence to suggest that your list of highly rated values is correct? Is the testimony from Chapter Three congruent with your list of core values? Do you notice behaviors or energies that reflect a value that you haven't already rated as important?

The next step of the exercise may be harder. What values are you conveying that you don't really hold and have not really intended to broadcast? For this determination, you need your friends. Try to find out what they see or hear that you haven't been seeing: differences between what you say and what you do or between ideas that you mean to express and what you actually say. We all have our blind spots. This feedback from others may help you clarify your values.

Working Out Conflicts and Incompatibilities Certain values are so important that we really do try to live our lives by them. Others we try to achieve "when possible." Reality may be forcing you in one direction, despite your intentions to move in another. Some values are in conflict with other values. This makes it impossible to live both values all of the time. One person we interviewed spoke of the conflict in terms of people skills that he values but abandons under performance pressures:

> I have people skills that a lot of CEOs would envy. But for a lifetime I've worked very hard and I've been very goal-focused, very task-oriented. . . . As deadlines become more critical and their importance becomes more apparent, I tend to close out the good human relations skills and just become so task-focused that . . . some of [the people I work with] probably feel like they're being hammered. Others feel like they're being excluded. Some probably feel like I don't care about them or their ideas or anything else. And they're probably right. . . . I need to be more conscious of what I'm doing and how I'm projecting myself.

Where do you see conflicts? For example, creativity and order are both wonderful values, but they often compete with each other. Creative work usually cannot be sequenced and scheduled. Similarly, other pairs of values are at odds for some people:

Loyalty (desire to serve under someone) versus recognition (desire to stand out)

Adventure (desire to explore) versus location (preference for a particular home site)

Status versus inner harmony

Autonomy versus affiliation

Competition versus collaboration

Fame versus spirituality

Look at your own set of prized values. Can you arrange any of them into "incompatible pairs"? If so, here are some ways that you might deal with the conflicts that you've discovered:

1. Decide which is more important to you. This doesn't mean that the "loser" is unimportant, only that it isn't quite as important to you, at this time of your life, as the "winner."

2. Ask yourself which of the two is more consistent with your actual behavior. If you don't like the answer, then you've got a somewhat larger problem.

3. If the first two steps don't lead to a decision, consider revising your definitions of these incompatible values. Perhaps you'll be able to find words that give each value a separate domain in your life. Maybe you have found that in fact they can be compatible in your life.

4. If nothing else works, admit that this pair of values may cause you trouble in some circumstances. Try to identify what those circumstances might be. If the conflict affects you at home, perhaps your spouse or partner can help you avoid the problem, deal with it for you, or assist you in coping when it arises. If the conflict centers at the office, then try to find a buddy there who will provide a similar kind of help.

Accommodating Changes over Time

One final question to think about is whether some of your core values may have changed over time. Core values tend to be relatively stable in a person's life, but their order of priority can certainly change. As we said earlier, what tops the list for someone at age thirty will almost certainly be different than what tops that person's list at age fifty-five. You might also change the amount of time you spend in relation to that value. For example, at one point in your life, achievement might be always valued; years later, you might not value it quite so much. Changes also occur in where and how a person demonstrates a value, perhaps moving it from a career or organizational setting into the domain of a personal hobby.

It could be fascinating to think about and categorize your values of ten years ago and compare them to your list today. Perhaps a spouse or longtime friend can give you insights in this regard and help you with the following questions.

What did you learn from this values exercise?

What surprised you?

Would you agree that your core values are the values listed in the always valued column?

Were you able to assign some values to the never valued column? Why are those values not important to you?

Do you see some incompatibilities in the columns?

Did you determine that values you thought were very important moved down on the list when you analyzed them against your actions?

VALUES, CONFLICTS, AND CAREERS

We noted earlier that there is no widely accepted list of values to which effective leaders all subscribe. But there are some things that matter about your specific values and the values of your organization in relation to your career as a leader. The two sets of values need to be in sync, not like the situation for this executive, who sees the value of taking risks:

> The company is not necessarily rewarding my kind of behavior. They talk a lot about taking risks, but they don't reward that behavior. They reward the success but not the risk. So if you take a risk and it doesn't quite work out, it's not always the best thing.

Here are four career necessities:

1. Understanding the traditional, current, and emerging core values in your field or a field in which you are thinking of working

2. Knowing which values are rewarded in your current or prospective organization

3. Being clear about the core values that you associate with your concept of the good leader

4. Knowing whether your personal core values match with items 1, 2, and 3

You can probably think of a number of ways to gather thoughts and information about item 1, the values common to your field. Also, organizations often have well-defined values. Leaders and managers who wish to work in those organizations need to verify that their own values are consistent with those of the organization. Many religious, research, academic, military, and governmental organizations have a kind of value base, often associated with well-defined rules and systems. One way would be to go through a sorting process similar to the process you conducted using Figure 4.1. You might use a similar process to explore your thoughts about item 2.

As organizational structures and climates change, some values become more appropriate than others, and overemphasizing a certain value that may have been fine in an earlier context generates conflict. For example, a very high value on autonomy isn't suitable in strong team environments that create or require strong interdependencies. Conflict often results when an individual in this environment can't become a "team player."

Many of our interviewees described values conflicts vis-à-vis their organization or that led to significant personal risk. Fortunately, their awareness of their own values generally kept them in contact with their principles and led them to decisions that did not damage their careers. Here are two case examples.

The first case involves a manager in an energy company who once reported directly to the president, for whom he was a valued troubleshooter. According to the manager, the president had "kind of brought me along with him. . . . I learned a lot from the man. He had a lot of raw, natural talent, very little formal or business training." But a conflict eventually arose as the president

> started exhibiting a very unethical side. . . . I would try to steer him away from these types of situations. Finally, one night I received a call from the chairman of the board, who asked me some very direct questions about things that were happening. I chose to be honest with him. As soon as we got off the phone, the president called and said, "I hear you just threw me to the wolves." . . .
>
> I didn't get fired, but it strained the relationship considerably. I stood up. I didn't back down. I wasn't apologetic. . . . The conflict was, on the one hand, wanting my security and taking care of my family and, on the other hand, sticking my neck out and trying to help the business.

In this case, we felt that the manager acted well. What allowed him to do so was his clarity about his own values, which gave him the strength to deal directly with both the chairman of the board and the president to whom the manager felt a personal debt.

The second case involves a financial officer who had worked for a while with a start-up that wasn't getting off the ground. He looked at two other possible jobs. Of the first he said:

> I thought it was a nice job, and I liked their values. I spent a lot of time, went to meetings, was really wooed. They had a problem that they needed to solve. I spent a great deal of time looking at their sense of purpose, corporate values, how they communicated with each other, worked in teams, and I thought this was great. They wanted to know about me, and I wanted to know about them too. [But] the decision-making process in this company takes a very long time.

Then suddenly, the second job came up:

It was a pre-IPO situation. I said, "Thank you, Lord, this is it!" I've always wanted to take a company public. I'd have a good title, comptroller, I'd be on the SEC report and all these wonderful things. I interviewed. The company was making money hand over fist. So I turned down the other company and said I'd take the position with the IPO.

The VP of finance was a Harvard grad, and I had a lot of respect for him. Then I interviewed with other people in the company. I had questions about some of the other people. They didn't seem as strong as I felt they should be, given the fact that this was going to be a public company under a lot of scrutiny, and there was tremendous risk.

Well, after going to work for them I found that the only people who had college degrees were people in the finance department. It took about three or four weeks to find out that this was part of the culture—that they devalued education and people who had education. There would be a lot of snide remarks about my boss for no other reason than that he had his Harvard degree. And when I talked about education, taking courses for myself, my staff, and so forth, I heard, "Well, we don't do that. We don't value education."

Then I went to staff meetings and saw how people operated. None of it was illegal, not something that would get you thrown in jail. But I was having a tremendous value clash here. I was thinking, "All your life you've stood for integrity and dealing with people below you fairly. . . . You're not going to be able to do that here. You're just going to have to take the money and not look after your people."

Finally, I just went back to the other company and said, "Is that job still open?" I did this just four weeks before the [second] company went public. I walked away from a lot of money. And that had been my whole goal in life: a whole lot of money.

I do have regrets, thinking, "Gee, you could have made a lot of money." I do [wish] I had the money for education for my kids and stuff. But what would you learn, [having] all those stock options but [being] in conflict every day? And would this organization hold that over me and manipulate me and make me unhappy? Probably. Or if not me, make my staff unhappy, and then I'd have to live with that.

Again, despite the element of regret, we think this person made the right choice in the long run, based on clear though sometimes opposing values.

Spend some time on these questions now.

What core values are prominent in your field?

Are your own core values similar?

Are your core values compatible with what the organization rewards?

Are the values you always or often value compatible with your organization's values?

What core values do you associate with good leadership?

Would others in your field and organization agree?

Do you hold core values that you see as compatible with leadership?

Which of your core values aren't compatible with leadership?

SUMMARY AND SYNTHESIS

There is debate about which values form the basis for effective leadership, but there is agreement that consistency in values and your ability to recognize and articulate the values you hold are important assets for you as a leader.

This chapter has led you through several exercises to identify your core values, test the congruence of your words and deeds, address potential incompatibilities and conflicts between your values, and relate your values to the context in which you work. We encourage you to continue talking with trusted colleagues, friends, and relations who can help you see your relationship to your values more clearly.

Based on the more formal work that you've already done in this chapter, try writing a brief statement of your current core values and any ongoing conflicts that you need to keep in mind.

Also take some time to analyze the alignment between your core values and the personal and leadership visions that you expressed in Chapter Three. Use the following pages or your personal journal.

1. Which core values are represented in your visions?

_____

_____

_____

_____

2. Does clarifying these values help eliminate some fogginess in your visions?

_____

_____

_____

_____

3. Are there values that you identified that are missing in your visions?

_____

_____

_____

_____

4. Do you see any conflicts between what you stated as your values and what you wrote for your personal vision and leadership vision? If so, in what ways will you reconcile the differences?

_____

_____

_____

_____

In Chapter Five, we'll ask you to look beyond your conscious values to other types of self-awareness. We will concentrate on your personal motivations, styles, competencies, responses to change, and other matters. Exploring these aspects of yourself will help you determine how well they support a decision to lead.

Get to Know Yourself as a Leader

Your leadership abilities flow from who you are as a person: your values, talents, styles, and self-image. The more aware you are of yourself in these respects, the more agile your behavior and the more effective your decisions will be.

This chapter is about authentic leadership; that is, leadership based not only on your vision and values but also on your own style and strengths. Just as it's possible for leaders to drift into a leadership role that doesn't fit their vision, they sometimes get into positions that don't allow them to work from their strengths. In some cases, leaders try to lead in the manner of a successful and adored predecessor, again not using their own authentic strengths and styles. Being authentic is about leading in a way that is natural for you and not trying to be someone else.

Authentic leadership also requires awareness of your own developmental needs and areas in need of change. Owning up to these developmental areas allows you to be more conscious of when things might not go well and how you can seek help from others.

The more thorough your self-awareness, the clearer you are about your motivations, your expectations of others, and your ways of relating, and the more flexible you will be in adjusting to new situations. Our emphasis on self-awareness is in line with advice given by insightful business consultant Richard Leider (1996): "Self-leadership is the basis of all leadership. It is based on knowing yourself and seeking reliable counsel. Leaders in a changing world need to take stock of their personal attributes that embrace or resist change" (p. 192).

This chapter will expand on the self-awareness work that you began by looking at your visions and values in Chapters Three and Four. In this chapter, you will examine motivations for leading, leadership competencies, preferred leadership roles, personal traits, learning capacity and styles, responses to change, and the career experience that you currently bring to leadership.

THE IMPORTANCE OF SELF-AWARENESS TO LEADERSHIP

Some years ago, Peter Vaill introduced the notion of management as a performing art, rather than simply as work that could be done by memorizing and applying formulas learned from books. Great managers use their whole selves, infusing their work with their own multifaceted, complex character and personality. Vaill (1989) wrote, "One mistake the arts would never make is to presume that a part or role can be exactly specified independent of the performer, yet this is an idea that has dominated work organizations for most of the twentieth century" (p. 124).

We believe that Vaill's idea about art and management also applies well to leadership. For some people, the "organic" connection between person and leader seems obvious. But it can take years to grow comfortable with the notion that strong leaders are the ones who are being themselves and acting in character as they fulfill their leadership roles. In fact, we believe that it is hard to be truly effective in any other way. A clear and honest understanding of your strengths and weaknesses allows you to make your leadership, your art, most useful to the organization.

Knowing yourself makes you more effective in working with others. It gives you insight into how your behavior affects them positively or negatively. It affords you a better understanding of yourself as a stimulus for influencing others. Do you put people at ease? Do you welcome their ideas? Self-awareness makes you better at gauging differences among people and treating them according to their emotional reactions. It also allows you to negotiate with others about difficult issues more skillfully and appropriately because you are secure in your knowledge about what's important and more likely to be cognizant of the thoughts and feelings of the people around you.

Knowing yourself enhances flexibility. You gain interpersonal agility and improve your awareness of how you can best contribute in various situations. You understand your style, your quirks, your shortcomings. You know better when to step forward and when to sit back and listen:

Self-aware and reflective executives do not simply accumulate knowledge and expertise; rather, they call upon the right capabilities at the right time. Such executives perform more effectively because they adapt better to the particular situation; they are more flexible. The more aware they are of what they can and can't do, the better able they are to deploy themselves in an enlightened way [Kaplan, Drath, and Kofodimos, 1991, p. 30].

Knowing yourself also gives you more confidence in the future you are planning for yourself. As we said earlier, self-awareness includes awareness of your visions and values. Being self-aware, you can more easily determine the approaches you wish to take in seeking this future picture as well as deal with the obstacles that come your way. With an extensive sense of who you are, you can better understand how failures build your learning.

Self-aware people know where they are headed and why; so, for example, they can be firm in turning down a job offer that is tempting financially but does not fit with deeper principles or long-term goals. People who lack self-awareness are apt to make poor decisions that tread on buried values and thereby bring on inner turmoil. "The money looked good, so I signed on," a colleague admits two years into a job, "but the work means so little to me that I'm constantly bored." The decisions of self-aware people mesh with their values; consequently, they often find work energizing. Writes one executive of long experience:

Only recently do I think I've come to understand leadership. That understanding, based on my own experience, has led me to some surprising conclusions, but I suspect others have had similar inklings. . . . The leadership journey is first and foremost an intensely personal one. I now believe it is impossible to define leadership without linking one's own life; the most important "Lost and Found Department" is inside [Brown, 1998, p. 9].

And there is much else in the literature that supports the notion that self-awareness is crucial for effective and personally satisfying leadership. For instance, Cashman (1998) calls leadership "authentic self-expression that creates value" (p. 20). We agree. We believe that you cannot effectively express who you are unless you know yourself well.

In their study of senior executives, Robert Kaplan, Wilfred Drath, and Joan Kofodimos (1991, pp. 45–46) furnish a list of the ways executives get themselves and their organizations in trouble through a lack of personal mastery and self-awareness:

Overreaching strategically

Being risk averse

Running roughshod over subordinates

Being cold and aloof

Focusing on empire building and other kinds of self-aggrandizement

Being inordinately concerned with getting ahead

Not distinguishing clearly enough between high- and low-priority items

Pushing themselves too hard and burning out

Pushing their people too hard and burning them out

Being rigid or difficult to influence

Being too concerned with status symbols, trappings of power, and the like

Not delegating enough (especially right after moving up to an executive job)

Having an inflated sense of their own importance

Distorting reality to create a favorable impression

Generally lacking integrity

The complement of knowing yourself is accepting what you know. By accepting who you are, including your limitations, you can acknowledge to yourself and others where you need help. You can also put together a developmental plan for working on your weaknesses or pair up with individuals who have compensating strengths.

YOUR PERSONAL LEADERSHIP PROFILE

How do you achieve self-awareness? Figure 5.1 delineates several areas that we think are important in coming to know yourself. We'll cover each area in the following pages. Reflecting on them will help you determine what you bring to leadership. Being aware of them should help you make better decisions about what leadership opportunities to take, seek, keep, or bypass.

Figure 5.1 Areas of Self-Awareness

- **Motivation to lead:** Validation, rewards, impact, service, meaning
- **Leadership competencies:** Building trust, forging teams, creating networks and alliances, possessing technological savvy, being comfortable with ambiguity and uncertainty, being flexible and agile, getting things done through others, reading organizational rhythms, communicating well, creating strategic vision
- **Preferred leadership roles:** Visionary, strategist, communicator, facilitator, integrator, nurturer, and others
- **Personal characteristics:** Leadership, energy, affability, dependability, resilience
- **Learning capacity and styles:** Learning from challenges, tactics for learning
- **Responses to change:** Overwhelmed, entrenched, BSer, or learner
- **Career history and lessons learned**

Each of us enters this process at our own individual level of understanding about who we are. If you've already participated in an assessment-for-development leadership program, you have a wide array of information about yourself to draw on that will enhance your reading of the following pages. Self-knowledge may also come from methods of self-exploration or organizational feedback, such as performance appraisals or 360-degree feedback. (The latter involves systematically collecting opinions about a manager's performance from a wide range of peers, subordinates, supervisors, customers, suppliers, and other knowledgeable parties.) If you picked up this book having done a lot of self-examination but never having had any formal feedback, this may be a good time to seek it.

YOUR MOTIVATION TO LEAD

Richard Leider (1998) identifies "three hungers" that are with us all our lives: "to connect deeply with a creative spirit, to know and express our gifts and talents, and to know that our lives matter" (p. 116). Perhaps he's right. Debate has continued for thousands of years about what really motivates people.

Borrowing Leider's three motives and adding some spin of our own, we offer the following five sources of leadership drive or motivation: personal validation, rewards, impact, service, and meaning. One or more of these sources will likely explain what is pushing you to be a leader. If this is a first at engaging in this self-exploration, take your time in reflecting on the various parts of this chapter.

Validation

One manager told us:

> Under the surface there's always been a bit of insecurity about whether or not I belong at the level I'm at. . . . As a result of this insecurity, I've been withholding part of myself in my business interactions, and that is actually seen as a problem.

Most people are concerned initially with whether they can be a leader at all or can be a leader in this organization. Will people follow their direction? Will they be accepted as a person of authority? Some people have received enough validation in earlier years and don't feel the need for further testing. Many others still want confirmation that they're on a productive path as leaders and not just carried away by their fantasies.

How to get that confirmation? If you are new to leadership, try experimenting in several leadership situations. You'll probably find that you can lead effectively, at least some of the time. The feeling of "I'm OK" may come in a flash or gradually, or perhaps with qualifications and some "developmental needs," but it's likely to be present in some degree. If you have been leading already, you may want to try new challenges that bring additional validation.

Rewards

By rewards we mean prestige, status, respect, inclusion, recognition, money, and other remuneration that typically accompany a leadership role to some degree. Because some people find the rewards of leadership to be quite important, these rewards can be powerful motivators.

Admitting to oneself or others that these are important is quite another matter, of course. Some people really are humble and don't much care about the perks. Others are so narcissistic that they fully expect such perks wherever they go. Among senior executives who have long enjoyed the rewards, some pay increasingly less attention to them, while others see them as an automatic, natural outcome of carrying the leadership burden. Very few feel guilty about them or uncomfortable with them.

A study of Generation Xers revealed that the top choices of nonmonetary rewards were training opportunities, exposure to decision-makers, credit for projects, increased responsibility, opportunities for creative expression, and control over their work schedules (Joyce, 1999). Do you know what rewards are important to you and how much of a driver they might be?

Impact

The urge to have impact, to make a difference, is powerful. One hears this constantly during hiring interviews: "I want to have impact. I want to see the results of my efforts." One young bank vice president describes the impact she wants to have in clear and measurable terms:

> Uniformity within the bank when it comes to groupware technologies—having a central place for the four hundred or so technical administrators throughout the bank to be able to come to know they're getting superior support, superior information. A pristine technology center is important to me, and getting a lot of respect from the people that ultimately come to us for guidance.

People who have an impact, who change things, who get things done, are granted a lot of respect in our culture. Being able to do this on a large scale, as a leader, is even better.

Most of us spend our early years in organizations learning how to get things done with what we have learned in school and on the job, making individual contributions in areas such as technology, finance, and marketing. Then perhaps we are chosen as supervisors. The first supervisory or managerial roles we get are seldom full time—often we start in such roles as crew chief, team leader, or "working manager" where there is still a strong individual contributor element.

Eventually we slip into a role in which our individual technical contribution is small, and our impact must come from being a leader. This is a very important transition. Not all new leaders like what they find when they get there; some elect to back out of these roles. Most professionals, however, find that they can shift gears and let go of their former ways of making an impact.

Leaders can have a very significant impact, of course, but quite different from that of the work of technical experts, craftsmen, salesmen, and other individual contributors. The leader's impact is typically accomplished through other people, and that's what makes it potentially more gratifying and more powerful. Here is how a leader who began her career in human resources describes an evolving view of impact:

> You start by [having an impact on] people at lower levels, just employees that need some help, that need to have someone in HR provide some guidance on a career perspective. I found that very satisfying earlier in my career. . . . When I got to a role more at the manager level, I started to get a little bit closer to understanding . . . what the business needs were and what the individual needs were. . . . Since then, I've really grown to be able to influence [other] managers, coming to the table with something to share and deliver.

Service

In Chapter Three, we quoted a retail industry manager whose leadership vision grew out of early experiences in sports. He expresses his leadership motivation mainly in terms of service:

> I lead from behind. I don't have a large ego; I don't consider myself needing the glory that comes with victories. I'd rather see myself with a group of people, behind a group of people, making it easier or possible for them to do the right thing.

To look back and see that we've helped others—that the world is a better place because we followed our vision and did our work—might be the ultimate reward of leadership.

An entire school of thought has developed around "servant leadership." Some individuals may not use these words but still express them in their leadership roles. This is often true of people who wish to be leaders in a "just cause," as in hospital or medical organizations, environmentalist groups, political campaigns, or government agencies. Service may also motivate a leader at the head of a population of worthy recipients, such as talented young women, fellow immigrants, or the people who live in one's home city.

Meaning

Some individuals seek leadership in order to find meaning for themselves and others. With increasing learning and development, one can gain greater clarity about life's meaning. Finding sense and meaning in life is a basic need. In fact, Wilfred Drath and Charles Palus (1994) say that "one thing we all share—across cultures, geography, and time—is the ability, and the hunger, to make things make sense" (p. 2). Success at this effort is extremely elusive and ever evolving. Particularly in the area of leadership, the context changes, our lives change, and the fast pace causes us to disregard data that will enable us to make meaning. But for individuals who are reflective and continuous learners, the motivation for making meaning continues to be a powerful drive in their leadership roles.

Synthesizing Motivation

Validation, rewards, impact, service, and meaning are possible sources of drive for leaders. You may find that one or more of them stands out for you. They give a sense of purpose, a rationale, a logic. When you have such a sense of what you're trying to accomplish, then you can see where leadership fits into your picture.

It is important to understand your leadership motivations as best you can. What gives you energy, direction, and reward as a person will also apply to your leadership behavior. In time, these forces can become the basis for the vision for an organization or community. The more significant your leadership role, the more influential your agenda will be. Can you answer these questions now?

What motivations drive your leadership vision?

How do you see these motivations operating in your current leadership role?

Where else do these motivations play out?

Is there something more you'd like to know about your own motives before you make leadership commitments?

YOUR LEADERSHIP COMPETENCIES

Beyond managerial decisions about broad goals and technical or financial issues, leadership means fostering the human spirit: creating relationships and systems that allow other people to get things done in an integrated, supported manner. To this end, we suggest that the following competencies are basic.

Building Trust

First comes building trust with people from varied backgrounds, specialties, work styles, genders, races, aspirations, and generations. If you want their best efforts, their best thinking, their passion for excellence, you must earn their trust and confidence. They will be far more impressed with your knowledge and ability than with your title. Some elements of trusting relationships are fairness, genuineness, willingness to learn from errors, and respect for each other's talents and needs.

Forging Teams

Teams are made out of individuals or groups with different skills and styles—and often conflicting agendas—sometimes working across geographical regions and time zones. Important team-building subskills include setting direction, understanding group cohesion, confronting conflict, giving feedback, and providing appropriate support and structure. Supporting the team as a whole as well as each individual member can be a tremendous task.

Creating Networks and Alliances

The executive director of a national nurses' organization told us:

> I've loved helping nurses get the education, . . . support, and networking that
> [they need to] feel good about the patient care that they give. The network
> of the people I know has really come to be one of my most important
> resources—putting the right people together in the right room so they can
> help each other. For me, leadership is building new networks all the time.

Networks and alliances are becoming more important than ever. Instead of building internal expertise, organizations are pairing up with other organizations that have that expertise. This requires the leaders in the organization to be skilled at creating, building, and maintaining these relationships. Having key networks and alliances within your organization is also crucial. These relationships allow you to share resources, support, data, and rumors (also important!). They are key for helping you stay "in the know" and are also useful for helping you understand how power and control may shift in complex and changing organizational environments. Relationships allow you to build up credits with people in useful places so that when you need help, you can cash in the credits and, ideally, get what you need; the relationships also allow others to do the same with you.

Possessing Technological Savvy

Working leaders of today can no longer distance themselves from technology. Technology is the way of the present and future. This ever-changing field and its many uses must be a part of the language and thoughts of leaders today. Technology is key to an organization's competitive, strategic, and operational direction and a driver of a person's individual success as well.

Being Comfortable with Ambiguity and Uncertainty

Uncertainty is inevitable, and ambiguity is ever present. You might want to cultivate this talent so much that you will prefer to work on the edges of stability and predictability, almost seeking out the ambiguous. Leadership is about navigating the gray area. To do this well requires trust between you and others, confidence in yourself, and a certain interpersonal agility.

Being Flexible and Agile

Leaders need to be able to respond to the unforeseen and make numerous decisions quickly. People who cannot handle simultaneous tasks or who need to "sit on" decisions until there's no chance for a mistake aren't candidates for leadership. Flexibility and agility also come into play with job assignments; constant changes thanks to mergers, buyouts, and restructuring create a strong probability that what you are doing now isn't what you will be doing eighteen months from now.

Getting Things Done Through Others

Almost nothing important gets done by just one person, especially by people in leadership roles. A leader needs patience with others and has to be comfortable with "political" problems and with sharing or giving away credit.

In our interviews, we asked the regional director of a national retail chain, "What do you think is the toughest job of a leader?" His immediate response:

> Patience with your people and patience with yourself. You might do something better than someone else, but three people can do it better and faster than you can. So you have to let them learn how to do it and let them understand how to do it.

He freely admitted that patience did not come naturally to him. He had to learn it as he went along.

> I think a leader who looks for glory, [who] is always out front of his people, gets frustrated in the leadership role because people recognize that and will not support that person in bad times. I've found that those kinds of [leaders] pass blame.

Reading Organizational Rhythms

Organizational rhythms reflect the readiness of a team or department to move forward, its investment in defensive routines, and its patterns of conflict avoidance. Sensing these rhythms involves knowing where energy is coming from, how power flows through the system, and the unwritten rules that govern the pulse of the group. A keen sense of rhythm may lead to success in risky ventures or when changing a traditional procedure.

Communicating Well

In light of all of the contextual changes described in Chapter Two (different organizational structures, different generations, more demanding customers, expanding technology), communication skills cannot be overemphasized. They include knowing the dos and don'ts of public speaking; videoconferencing, teleconferencing; written communications (memos, e-mail, discussions on the Internet); and of course listening. People who can communicate well will more likely succeed in leadership posts. Flexible and widely dispersed organizations place a premium on being heard and understood.

Creating Strategic Vision

Strategic vision is the most difficult and least understood competency. It means looking into the future, seeing the possibilities, and making a vision tangible to your colleagues. In organizations moving at ever-faster speeds and seeking new directions, defining a vision of the future is extremely challenging. Actually selling that vision to others is even harder.

Synthesizing Competencies

Is our list of competencies complete? Certainly not. But it's a good beginning.

Would you add any other competencies to the list of leadership skills?

Which competencies do you definitely possess?

Which are not strong points of yours?

What have you done to develop those areas in which you are weak?

Which competencies should you be working harder to improve?

What are the most important competencies in your current role?

YOUR LEADERSHIP ROLES

In using various leadership competencies, executives actually perform a variety of leadership roles. The importance of these roles differs with the situation and the challenges at hand. Their definitions may also change from one organization to another. Having the ability to recognize, span, use, and develop these roles is crucial to leadership. All contribute importantly to the work of organizations.

The roles most frequently discussed by practicing leaders are the following:

Visionary	Strategist	Communicator	Team or community builder
Learner	Integrator	Motivator	Astute global observer
Facilitator	Mediator	Problem solver	Negotiator
Nurturer	Risk taker	People developer	Change agent

What other roles come to mind that aren't on this list? Write them down. Then pick the three roles that you do best. Which three are most difficult for you? How do your responses align with your core values in Chapter Four? Are you seeing some patterns? Also consider the following further questions about roles.

Which of your three best roles are integral to your work?

How well do you perform these three roles?

Which roles are rewarded in your organization?

Which roles do you value most?

Which roles are you being asked to play by your boss and direct reports?

For roles you don't play well, are there individuals from whom you can learn?

In your organization, which roles need further development?

Here's a good exercise for looking further at your roles. Read the following numbered statements. For each one, decide whether it is currently one of your strengths (S), something that you need to develop (D), or a capacity about which you lack sufficient information and therefore don't know where to place (DK). Write S, D, or DK beside each statement.

We have noted correspondences between the statements and our earlier list of roles, but these are not validated by any research process. Each statement merely describes what a behavior for that role might look like. We intend the statements as triggers for helping you investigate what roles you play in organizations and how effective you think you are. To get more accurate feedback, you might want to assess yourself more formally with a 360-degree feedback instrument.

_____ 1. I can develop a vision for my department, business line, role, and so forth, in the organization. (visionary)

_____ 2. I can translate strategy into action. (strategist)

_____ 3. I can link my leadership responsibilities to the mission of the organization. (strategist)

_____ 4. I can effectively create significant organizational change. (change agent)

_____ 5. I can effectively implement change in my organization. (change agent)

_____ 6. I can get things done despite resistance in the organization. (change agent)

_____ 7. I learn from my own experience. (learner)

_____ 8. I can communicate that vision to others in the organization. (communicator)

_____ 9. When working with peers from other functions or units, I can gain their cooperation and support. (integrator)

_____ 10. I can bring together individuals from across the organization to solve problems. (integrator, facilitator)

_____ 11. I am often called on to mediate among people in the organization. (facilitator, mediator)

_____ 12. I can bring people together successfully around tasks. (team builder)

_____ 13. I can build warm, cooperative relationships with others. (team builder)

_____ 14. I can pull people together around a common goal. (team builder)

_____ 15. I am a good coach and counselor. (nurturer)

_____ 16. I possess a personality that puts people at ease. (nurturer)

____ **17.** I take advantage of opportunities to do new things. (risk taker)

____ **18.** I am willing to act when others hesitate or just talk. (risk taker)

____ **19.** I set a challenging environment to encourage individual growth. (people developer)

____ **20.** I provide constructive feedback to other people in order to assist in their development. (people developer)

____ **21.** I think in terms of options and look for win-win situations. (negotiator)

____ **22.** I can inspire and motivate people to action. (motivator)

____ **23.** I am someone others seek out for assistance in solving problems. (problem solver)

____ **24.** I have worked extensively in international arenas and can navigate different cultural norms. (astute global observer)

____ **25.** I am sensitive to differences among cultures. (astute global observer)

Do you see any patterns in what you do well?

Do you see blind spots?

Are there items in your "don't know" category?

Are these things that you would agree are important?

Do you see connections to roles that you might play?

Do you favor some roles over others?

Can you get feedback from a colleague, friend, or partner about how you perform in these roles?

YOUR PERSONAL CHARACTERISTICS

So far in this chapter, you have reflected on motivations for leading, leadership competencies, and leadership roles. To continue to expand your thinking about how you lead, let's take a look at some positive and negative characteristics often associated with leadership.

Figure 5.2 presents five broad categories of personal characteristics that are related to the demands of leadership. In each category except one, specific characteristics are listed. The categories and specific traits are derived from a psychometric instrument, the Campbell Leadership Index (Campbell, 1998).

Figure 5.2 Personal Characteristics
Related to Leadership Qualities

Quality	Characteristics
Leadership: The act of being out in front, making new and creative things happen	**Ambitious:** Competitive, forceful, determined to make progress **Daring:** Adventuresome, willing to try new experiences, risk-oriented **Dynamic:** Enthusiastic, takes charge, inspires others, seen as a leader **Enterprising:** Resourceful, works well with the complexities of change **Experienced:** Savvy, well connected, well informed **Farsighted:** Insightful, forward-looking, visionary **Original:** Creative, imaginative, sees the world differently, has new ideas **Persuasive:** Convincing, fluent, articulate, persuasive
Energy: Possessing the physical strength, endurance, acuity, and other physical attributes required for sustained leadership work	
Affability: A combination of qualities that enable leaders to foster teamwork and cooperation and make people feel valued	**Affectionate:** Warm, expressive, close, nurturing **Considerate:** Cooperative, helpful, thoughtful, willing to work with others **Empowering:** Encouraging, supportive, motivates and helps others to achieve **Entertaining:** Extroverted, humorous, outgoing, amusing **Friendly:** Cheerful, likable, pleasant to be around, smiles easily

Figure 5.2 Personal Characteristics
Related to Leadership Qualities, Cont'd.

Quality	Characteristics
Dependability: Personal credibility and the ability to allocate organizational resources and manage details	**Credible:** Candid, trustworthy **Organized:** Orderly, methodical, plans ahead and follows through **Productive:** Dependable, effective, uses time and resources well **Thrifty:** Frugal, not extravagant or wasteful of resources
Resilience: The ability to show optimism, mental durability, and emotional balance	**Calm:** Easygoing, serene, unhurried, unruffled **Flexible:** Adaptable, not stubborn, adjusts easily to changes **Optimistic:** Positive, handles difficulties without becoming discouraged **Trusting:** Trusts and believes in others, not cynical

Source: Campbell, 1998. Used by permission.

Receiving high ratings on these traits does not ensure effective leadership, but it does indicate a propensity to exhibit good leadership.

Reflect on the twenty-one specific characteristics that are listed under the categories, as well as the energy category as a characteristic in itself. From these twenty-two possibilities, choose six to eight that you think describe you very well. How does each contribute to your effectiveness? Choose another six to eight that you believe do not describe you very well. Are these qualities that you want to work on? Write down some clear examples as evidence for both sets of lists.

Do you see connections between the values you examined in Chapter Four (pages 60–61) and the leadership characteristics you chose from Figure 5.2? For example, in Chapter Four, perhaps you rated *advancement* as always valued. Did you also now choose *ambitious* in Figure 5.2? Here are some other possible matches:

Value	Characteristic
Affiliation	Friendly
Activity	Productive
Enjoyment	Entertaining
Courage	Daring
Knowledge	Experienced

You will probably see other connections. Take a moment to see what lessons you can glean from looking at both lists. Record your discoveries.

_____

_____

_____

_____

YOUR CAPACITY TO LEARN AND YOUR LEARNING STYLES

From intensive research at the Center for Creative Leadership, we know that learning is essential to leadership (Lombardo, McCall, and Morrison, 1988). How do we learn? Most often by reflecting on experiences we have on the job. Some executives embrace learning with a passion and are eager to know everything. Warren Bennis and Burt Nanus (1985), in their study of ninety top leaders, indicate that "nearly all leaders are highly proficient in learning from experience" (p. 188). Let's look at what situations give you the best opportunities to learn.

Challenge and Learning

In *Eighty-Eight Assignments for Development in Place*, Michael Lombardo and Robert Eichinger (1989, pp. 5–7) highlight eleven challenges that are common to an executive's learning experience. They have found that for an experience to be valuable for learning (or development), five or more of the following eleven challenges have to be present:

1. The person is managing a situation where there is both a clear measure of success and the possibility of failure.

2. The situation requires aggressive action, take-charge leadership.

3. The situation involves working with new people or a lot of people.

4. The situation creates additional personal pressure.

5. The situation requires influencing people, activities, and factors over which there is no direct authority.

6. The situation involves high levels of variety, ambiguity, and uncertainty.

7. The situation is closely watched by people whose opinions count.

8. The situation requires building a team, starting something from scratch, or fixing or turning around something in trouble.

9. The situation has a major strategic component and is intellectually challenging.

10. The person interacts with an especially good or bad boss.

11. The person is working where something important is missing (for instance, authority, skills, support, credentials).

Being aware of these types of challenges can help you become more conscious of what you are learning from these challenges as well as help you identify opportunities, assignments, or experiences in which they are present. Right now, consider several related questions.

Does your current or prospective leadership role include some of the eleven challenges?

How and what are these challenges currently helping you learn?

Do you have too much, too little, or the wrong kind of challenge?

Are you willing to stretch yourself so that learning can take place?

Learning Styles

Other research from the Center for Creative Leadership has shown that you learn the most if you employ a variety of approaches or tactics to the task of learning (Dalton, 1998). Using different learning tactics makes you a more versatile learner, gleaning more from every developmental experience. It's important to know what kinds of learning tactics you use because your way of learning becomes an important factor in how you lead. In fact, in this world of fast-paced change, leading well is all about learning.

Let's examine four sets of tactics related to feeling, acting, thinking, and accessing others. First you'll need to understand where your preferences lie amongst the four. Then you may need to expand from your preferred, more comfortable tactics to others. The result can be greater effectiveness as a leader.

Feeling tactics. Individuals who learn by using feeling tactics are able to manage the anxiety and uncertainty that comes with new challenges. They can acknowledge the impact of their feelings on what they do, trust what their intuition is telling them, and confront themselves when they know they are avoiding a challenge.

Action tactics. Individuals who use action tactics learn by doing. They confront a challenge head-on and hands-on, in real time, and figure it out as they go along. The action tactician is a risk taker, a person who gets down on the factory floor and makes on-the-spot decisions in a crunch.

Thinking tactics. Individuals who learn through thinking tactics work things out by themselves. They recall similar or contrasting situations. They imagine the future and play out scenarios. They gather information from books and reports to ground themselves well in the facts. These individuals don't take chances that they will be caught uninformed.

Tactics based on accessing others. Individuals who learn by accessing others seek advice, examples, support, or instruction from people who have met a challenge similar to the one they face. They also learn how to do something by watching someone else do it or by taking a formal course or program that addresses their needs.

Use the following sets of statements to identify your preferred learning tactics. Mark the statements that apply to you. Then read on about interpretation.

Feeling Tactics
When facing a challenging opportunity, I . . .

___ carefully consider how I feel

___ confront myself if I am avoiding the challenge

___ carefully consider how others might feel

____ trust my feelings about what to do

____ acknowledge the impact of my feelings on what I decide to do

Action Tactics
When facing a challenging opportunity, I . . .

____ figure it out by trial and error

____ allow my own experience to be my guide

____ immerse myself in the situation to figure it out quickly

____ don't allow lack of information or input to keep me from making my move

____ commit myself to making something happen

Thinking Tactics
When facing a challenging opportunity, I . . .

____ regularly turn to magazine articles, books, or the Internet for knowledge or information

____ ask myself, "How is this similar to other things I know?"

____ imagine how different options might play out

____ try to conceptualize what the ideal person would do

____ try to rehearse my actions mentally before entering the situation

Tactics Based on Accessing Others
When facing a challenging opportunity, I . . .

____ often seek the advice of the people around me

____ look for role models and try to emulate their behavior

____ find someone who can give me feedback about how I am doing

____ look for a course or training experience

____ look for someone who has had experience in that area

The set in which you marked the greatest number of statements represents your primary learning tactic. You may have more than one. If you use only one or two tactics, it is possible that you are overusing or misusing these tactics. Or you may be avoiding situations in which other tactics are needed. The most versatile learners use all four tactics.

Now ask yourself a few questions about your responses.

How broad is your current range of learning tactics?

Do you depend on one set much more than the others?

Does your current pattern impose limitations?

Has this pattern gotten you into trouble in the past?

Do you have the motivation to add one or more of the less favored tactics to your repertoire?

What demands would change make on your patience or fortitude? What discomfort might be involved?

If you want to stay put in the style of learning that you're familiar with even though it doesn't garner developmental or career rewards for you, consider that stance before you undertake a new leadership role.

YOUR RESPONSES TO CHANGE

By this point in the chapter, you've already gleaned a lot of important insight about yourself. Let us move on to the question of how you deal with change.

The workplace is not what it once was in terms of the relationship between leaders and their organization. Layoffs are common, mergers turn company cultures upside down, new partnerships and affiliations require new attitudes toward leadership, and restructuring makes once familiar organizations unrecognizable. First let's look at three general observations about the experience of change. Then we'll ask you to consider four ways in which you yourself may respond to change.

Three Realities of Change

Change causes stress. Always. This is true whether the change is positive or negative, planned or unexpected, small or large, private or shared. Change typically involves a loss, or at least a risk of losing something important. Change means moving into an unknown future, reshuffling the cards, developing new habits and methods, creating systems, working with different people, and playing by different rules. It shifts existing comfort zones that people have come to rely on.

People don't like stress and try to minimize it—sometimes in unproductive ways by denying the importance of change, by hurrying through or avoiding changes, or by blaming someone for not managing things well. If you doubt the truth of this, think back to an important change you underwent: a wedding, a divorce, a change of lifestyle or diet that your doctor ordered, a move, a lost job.

We need to be prepared to deal with stress whenever there is change. As you take on and move through leadership roles, you need to be prepared to deal with increasing amounts of it in yourself and others. Try as best you can to avoid the unproductive ways of dealing with it.

Change and continuity need to be integrated. The popular and business press these days harps on how important it is to manage change well. Dire consequences are predicted for the person or organization that fails to change quickly and often. That may be so, but it's not the entire story. We believe that it is also important to maintain continuity in your identity, values, purposes, and history throughout the process of change. The successful leader is the one who does this well.

Someone who experiences a lot of change in a leadership role doesn't cease being the person he or she has been. Some old habits are left behind, and new ones are adopted. But there is more continuity than there is difference in that person during the process of change.

Change is resisted. Unfortunately, there's a widespread misconception that the leader's job is to overcome resistance to change—to make everyone enthusiastic about every change or to get rid of people who throw up roadblocks. Similarly, there's a misconception that the person who successfully grows and develops is the one who has the willpower to let go of the "old stuff" and move on to the golden future unencumbered. We do not subscribe to these views.

Resistance to change is natural, healthy, and valuable. It is actually a good way to send information from the "changee" to the "changer." If you are leading a change, resistance might alert you to important things that should be kept or modified rather than abandoned completely. Resistance tells you what must be done to make the transition smooth and effective. It tells you where you need to focus your attention as a leader. It points up values, history, and cultural characteristics that shouldn't be casually discarded. It's important to understand where resistance is coming from and to appreciate it rather than dismiss it as bad or inconsequential.

Part of the art of leading change is learning to decipher the "resistance code." Resistance is almost always expressed inarticulately, wrapped in several layers of emotions. This is true whether the changes are occurring in a person, a family, a work team, or an entire organization or culture. Dealing with these changes calls for patience, affection, practice, and lots of conversation.

Four Responses to Change

Kerry Bunker (1994) and David Noer (1997) have come up with a way of thinking about how individuals respond to change. Noer says, "As the old psychological contract between individual and organization continues to unravel, many of us are struggling with basic questions such as how to lead, motivate, and plan in this uncharted new environment where, like it or not, we are all temporary employees" (p. 6).

Almost anyone who joins the leadership ranks or is already a member will have to deal with some momentous changes during his or her career. Some will sail through; others will be felled by layoffs and restructurings. Many more will drift in a state of paralysis, waiting to be rescued. How well you respond to change is a part of who you are and how you lead.

In their work at CCL with executives undergoing major job changes, Bunker (1994) and Noer (1997) identified four primary behavioral responses. The individuals who display them can be characterized as the overwhelmed, the entrenched, the BSers, and the learners. As we examine these individuals' responses, reflect on how you have dealt with change in the past and how you might react in the future.

The Overwhelmed These individuals understand the nature of the change they are undergoing but can't let go of the old ways. Instead they exhibit a litany of behaviors. They withdraw and avoid. Noer says that they are somewhere between unhappy and depressed. A typical description of this type is, "She doesn't have any energy; she seems flat." They're also frustrated and anxious because they don't know how they fit in. Their self-esteem is bruised. The overwhelmed are professional victims. By withdrawing, they give up their organizational power and their power over themselves.

The primary coping strategy of the overwhelmed is to block out both what is changing in the organization and what is changing in themselves. They retreat into old patterns that they think are safe. They spend their energy avoiding reality. They are in deep denial that their jobs might be over, that the organization is not the same warm and fuzzy place they are used to, or that restructuring is taking place.

The Entrenched These individuals are able to learn and change in the face of workplace transitions, but they have a hard time doing it. Their primary coping mechanism is to perform the work in a narrow and limited manner. Unlike the overwhelmed, the entrenched can be productive; but they often insist on doing things in the same old way, which can circumscribe their contributions severely.

Limited in their ability to change, the entrenched are frustrated and angry. They tend to overidentify with the organization's past, and lecture their co-workers on how things used to be. This is a screen to protect themselves from taking on the new transition in a healthy way. They tend to blame, complain, resist, and work hard at previously successful behavior that is not appropriate for the current situation. They try to ride out the crisis.

Noer (1997, p. 50) quotes one individual describing an entrenched worker this way: "He keeps telling me that 'we are forgetting what made us who we are.' He really takes the change personally."

The BSers BSers appear comfortable with change but are really fooling everybody. They don't display the fear of the overwhelmed and entrenched, but neither do they take substantive action in response to change. A typical comment about a BSer is, "None of this seems to bother him. Does he understand what's going on?"

BSers take on the challenge, but they don't give it much thought, and they want it to be over quickly. They are confident that they can handle any crisis with aggressive shooting from the hip. They're often impatient with the confusion and whining of their co-workers.

One of a BSer's first reactions in times of change is to jockey overconfidently for a position of influence. Anxious to do something—anything—the BSer presses for quick action. Appearing in control, a BSer can fool the boss for a very long time.

The Learners Learners respond actively to change. They are the ones who tend to hold the organization together through transitions. They possess self-confidence and optimism and are able to learn from experience and apply their skills to various situations. They engage the challenge and grow from it.

Learners face the issues and work hard for positive outcomes. They certainly reflect on the challenges at hand and the difficulties confronting the organization, but they plunge ahead looking for the best possible outcomes. They accept that they need to let go of the old, and they take action in the face of uncertainty. Others might describe the learner as "a cool customer. She knows what we've got to do, accepts it, and gets on with it."

Learners are not deterred by short-term setbacks. In fact, they tend to find the silver linings and employ humor in their workday situations. They are willing to stretch outside their comfort zones in pursuit of a goal. They aren't Pollyannas. They are sober, responsible individuals who are blessed with the inner resources of a positive outlook and a can-do attitude. They do best in times of change.

At various times, each of us may exhibit all of these responses to change. But one response may be more typical than others. Think about the following questions. Keep checking to see if you have changed your responses as you progress through your leadership career.

How proactively do you handle the stress of change?

Do you have ways of integrating change with continuity in who you are?

How effectively do you read and use resistance?

How well do you decode your own and other people's reactions to change?

What is your typical response to change?

How does this affect the quality of your leadership?

How might you further develop a learner's response to change?

CAREER HISTORY AND LESSONS LEARNED

Against the accumulating overview of motivations, competencies, roles, characteristics, and styles, let's now look at your career history and the various positions you have held. The purpose is to examine what you have learned and how this informs your leadership. Most of your learning about leadership comes not from books but from working with people in an organizational setting. The Center for Creative Leadership has spent many years documenting that most executives learn primarily at their desk, right on the job (Lombardo, McCall, and Morrison, 1988). These are the most important experiences you will have, and they will tell you what you like and don't like about leadership.

You may want to take some notes or write at length in a journal as you work through the following steps.

First, examine your career progression from day one. What decisions led you from one position to the next? How proactive were you in seeking new opportunities? Did you ever "ride the sea of change" and later regret taking a position? Do you regret not taking something that was available to you? At what point in your career were you most satisfied? What were you doing? When have you been least satisfied?

Next, describe the leadership components of each position you have held. Were you a change agent, a nurturer? What specific leadership lessons did you learn along the way? What did you like most about performing a certain leadership role? What did you like least? What are the leadership components of your current role? What would help you be more successful at doing these well? What would you like to do more of? Less of?

Next, focus on some key leadership experiences. Describe four leadership challenges in which you had the greatest impact. Consider also the impact of others who were working around you. How did you know you had an impact? What makes these career moments memorable for you? What did they teach you about yourself?

What leadership experiences are missing from your career history? Should you try to incorporate any of them? What significance could they have in your career progression?

Asked these kinds of questions, the managers we interviewed offered refreshing insights and confessions. Said one, "I think the things I've done were more managerial than truly leadership." Said another:

> I've learned that I'm not comfortable taking risks. It's just not in my comfort zone, and it's something I need to continue to challenge. Also, I don't like conflict. . . . I like to build a relationship, and I'm really good at team building and motivating. . . . I'm good at . . . setting a vision, setting some direction without micromanaging. . . . But I don't like to deal with conflict, and sometimes I need to push back.

Of course, each individual made unique discoveries. In contrast to the relatively restrained individual we just quoted, another person offered these responses:

Companies tend to throw you into that management spot. I got there because I was a great technician, not because they saw me exhibiting great management skills. . . . It was a good two to three years before I started feeling somewhat comfortable at being the manager. Suddenly every decision I made not only affected me but ten or twelve other people. . . . I think one of the most difficult things was to learn those people skills and be comfortable confronting people on performance issues and those kinds of things.

My personality tends to be very strong. I think it's good, and I want the rewards. But I want to be very careful that . . . I'm not in this just for me. We've got a group that has to survive here. If I keep getting promoted up the ladder and my team is staying where [it was], then I don't feel like I've succeeded. Is it a discomfort for me to have the limelight? Not in a million years, but I'd feel even better if they were with me.

Consider a more extended example of how another person's career history has shown her the place of leadership in her life.

Approaching thirty-five, Kathy Meadows (a fictional name) is young, sharp, creative, and eager to be productive—many things that any organization would want. Her M.B.A. rests on top of good entrepreneurial and consulting experience. From an early age, she's successfully led projects and small businesses. Her peers in the M.B.A. "case study" exercise called her "a natural" to be the head of the team.

Her first post–M.B.A. full-time job was in a staff role. Her frustration was clearly evident: her good ideas went into cyberspace or the wastebasket—management wasn't inclined to listen to a good-looking upstart with potential. They expected her to help them succeed; she wanted them to help her succeed. It didn't last long.

Off she went to do something where she could be in charge, build something. She took on a sales role, opening a new branch in a high-risk move for a company. She made it work, and the company added staff and scope to her job. Soon she found herself "leading" the national business development effort, reporting directly to the marketing vice president while still in her early thirties.

She soon found that she had to make an important decision about where her career should go next. She felt that she could continue along this path or move into the company's mainstream work. The company's services were inherently more interesting to her than even the top sales job would be. If she waited any longer, she wouldn't be able to afford the switch, which even now would call for a freeze in her income for a couple of years.

Deciding to leave the marketing department, Kathy has arranged for a transfer. She feels that she has demonstrated her leadership competencies—to herself and to the others—and is confident that she can come back to them. As a practical career matter, she realizes that if she is ever to become one of the most senior leaders in the company, she needs to validate herself in its mainstream professional services—now.

Most important, Kathy's vision for herself is that she be a professional at what the company does and only secondarily a leader, a salesperson, or anything else. Making that vision "crystal clear," as she describes it, was the turning point. There's leadership in there too, but only on the basis of being a professional first.

SUMMARY AND SYNTHESIS

This chapter focused on the role of self-awareness in allowing you to become a more authentic leader. In addition to reviewing your on-the-job learning, it asked you to look at your motivation to lead, leadership competencies, leadership roles, personal traits, and styles of dealing with learning and change.

1. Look back over your responses throughout the chapter. Make a copy of Figure 5.1, go back to the notes you have been taking, and circle the words that were most descriptive of you. Do you see any relationships between the leadership competencies, leadership roles, and personal characteristics that you believe describe you? What about any patterns in the areas you believe to be weak? What are these patterns and relationships, and what insights do you gain from them?

_____

_____

_____

_____

_____

2. What other patterns do you see as you have captured information about yourself throughout the various sections of this chapter?

_____

_____

_____

_____

3. Does your current or prospective leadership position reinforce what you believe
you do well? Does it ask for the kind of leader that you are and want to be?

_____

_____

_____

_____

4. Do you find yourself in or seeking a position for which you may not be
equipped?

_____

_____

_____

_____

In the next chapter, we will visit the fifth and final topic in the framework of
this book: balance among the various components of your life. Relying on your
increased awareness of vision, values, and leadership strengths and weaknesses,
you will explore strategies for achieving a more integrated and rewarding life in
which leadership plays a significant part.

Balance Your Work Life and Your Personal Life

This chapter is about achieving the right balance of focus, energy, and time between your work as a leader and the other important areas of your life. Achieving this balance is a challenge.

One CEO commented, "I hate the balance concept because it means that every day I'm going to be a perfect mom and a perfect chief executive. Impossible. Simply impossible."

We agree completely. Balance cannot be about perfection. Personal balance isn't easy to achieve, and it's important to be realistic about it. Avoid the trap of thinking that only perfection will do.

Nor do we advocate the typically unrealistic idea of equal time for work and nonwork. We take balance to mean making decisions about how different activities and areas of your life are weighted to the right degree for you at each unique point in your life. Each person's solution is different.

This chapter covers strategies for achieving balance. Our discussions of mastery, intimacy, parenting, and other variables connected to your life outside of work should also assist your thinking about the place of leadership in your overall life.

THE IMPORTANCE OF BALANCE TO LEADERSHIP

Some younger leaders of the baby bust generation seem to be doing what many baby boomers only talk about. They're not buying in to the same traditional constraints as often as the boomers have done (who in turn have been less constrained than many members of the Depression Era and World War II generation). They demand more flexibility, more choices, and fewer trade-offs. As mentioned in Chapter Five, one of the top nonmonetary rewards among twenty-somethings is control over their work schedule (Joyce, 1999). But even this control does not necessarily mean that balance has been achieved.

No one we interviewed and no executive we've ever worked with has been immune to imbalance. We each have many days when we feel like a fiddler on the roof, standing at a precarious angle, swaying back and forth as we try to make beautiful music in the midst of turmoil. Long hours, tiring travel, and the twenty-four-hour on-call responsibilities of organizations conspire to deny managers a sense of being in control of all of the areas of life. The stress of work hounds them even on weekends and holidays, taking mental energies that are needed for relieving stress.

As your leadership work becomes more important to you and to the organization, you tend to find less time for everything else. Conflicts between work and family are often the leading concern expressed by executives in leadership roles. One of life's unkindnesses is that the tasks of building a family and building a career occur simultaneously for many people.

Balance is also an issue for single executives. Organizations often assume that single people can take on more work, more travel, and longer workdays—forgetting that single people have personal lives too.

But why is balance essential? Because imbalance usually leads to a loss of energy, and leadership requires abundant energy—more than enough to share with others! It's really the combination of balance and focus (the alignment of vision, values, and actions discussed in earlier chapters) that gives a person the energy not only to do the job but to invigorate others as well.

Without balance and focus, your energy will fade over the long haul; the stamina won't be there to overcome real obstacles. Instead, you'll discover stress, burnout, boredom, conflict, and other frustrating symptoms, as this executive did:

> I was involved in so many different things that I really didn't have any time for myself. I lost sight of who I was. I got to a point where I was just getting up every day, and people would wind me up and I'd just go. I didn't know what day it was, where I was supposed to be. It was like I was driven by an appointment book. So I had to shut down. I actually shut down for about six months before I started getting reenergized and back into activities.

By contrast, when your life is focused and balanced, you see ways to achieve your ends, and energy can flow. Thus your effectiveness as a leader depends in part on your ability to balance or integrate your career and family involvements, your community and social lives, the pursuit of learning, and whatever else you choose to do in life. Each part of life makes legitimate demands; each offers important nourishment; your actions in each affect what you can do in the others. Balance lets you lead with full heart and soul. Effective use of your whole self allows you to go beyond "techniques" of leadership.

Does Balanced Mean Better?

Are balanced leaders better performers? There is reason to think so. At the Center for Creative Leadership, we use many assessment instruments, two of which have specific items about balance. On the *SKILLSCOPE* questionnaire (Kaplan, 1997, p. 3), the item is: "Strikes a reasonable balance between his/her work life and private life." On *Benchmarks* (Lombardo and McCauley, 2000, p. 26), the scale titled "Balance Between Personal Life and Work" features these four items:

1. Acts as if there is more to life than just having a career.
2. Has activities and interests outside of career.
3. Does not take career so seriously that his/her personal life suffers.
4. Does not let job demands cause family problems.

In administering these instruments thousands of times, we have found that when executives received high marks from their co-workers on these specific items about balance, the high marks on balance did not coincide with low marks on performance. The executives were considered productive, proactive leaders of the organization despite the time they carved out for their family, community, or other external endeavors.

In research on women conducted at the Center for Creative Leadership, we have found that multiple roles nourish rather than hinder career. One study of 222 high-achieving managerial women (Ruderman, Ohlott, Panzer, and King, 1999) showed that commitment to four key roles (home care, parental, marital, and occupational) was related to enhanced work performance as well as to life satisfaction and self-esteem. Women committed to multiple roles were rated higher by bosses, peers, and direct reports on organizational skills, interpersonal skills, and personal awareness than women committed to single roles. Moreover, single-minded devotion to work correlated with poor collaboration and placing undue pressure on co-workers.

The Organizational View

Organizations, departments, and the people within them vary in terms of their attention to this issue, but many organizations are aware of a leader's need for balance and reflect this awareness in various ways.

Organizational preference for balanced leaders is starting to show up in recruitment, both because balance is seen as a desirable quality and because paying attention to balance issues is likely to help the organization retain high-caliber leaders in whom they make large investments.

In some organizations, if you were a fly on the wall in upper-level hiring discussions you'd hear lots of talk with no apparent connection to the leadership job itself. Conversing among themselves or with professional recruiters, hiring executives stray far from the measurable knowledge and skills that lawyers and human resource specialists tell them to stick to. They talk at length about balance in a candidate's life; about physical and mental health; about sense of humor, charm, and the ability to show "presence and poise" in various communities. They talk about family relationships and supports. You might also hear about candidates' abilities to have fun, find time for community service, or be a good parent, despite other demands on their time. Not all of these topics come up every time, but they are much more common than they used to be in the inner circles where leaders are sought.

Beyond traditional methods of developing leaders (through on-the-job and academic experiences), some organizations have added methods for dealing with the leader as a more complex, more integrated person who should bring a "total person" approach to work. Some organizations support attendance at self-assessment leadership programs that deal directly with reviewing, understanding, and integrating yourself and your life space. Other company-sponsored programs focus on spiritual examination. Some programs are based on outdoor exercises that build confidence and courage. Still other programs let leaders explore the great intellectual and literary traditions of the world. There are even programs for husband-wife or total-family participation in pursuit of a fuller integration of interests.

> Do you think balance is important to leadership?
>
> Does your current organization acknowledge balance as a positive thing? In what ways?
>
> Are you in a position to acknowledge balance as a positive thing for employees who report to you?

INTERACTIONS BETWEEN WORK AND OTHER AREAS

There are positive opportunities implicit in the challenge of balance. One type of opportunity lies in the fact that there are important benefits and lessons to be learned and transferred from one area of your life to another.

Impact of Work on Personal Lives

Many of the leaders we interviewed described positive effects of work life on their personal lives. They often mentioned the financial rewards of individual advancement: access to "the good things" in their personal lives—the kind of family and home they really wanted, children's education, and so forth. For some this also included opportunities to travel to interesting parts of the world and the chance to integrate business trips with family vacations in special places. Some interviewees also mentioned opportunities to have lots of interesting friends and acquaintances and the ability to call on these networks when needed.

Impact of Personal Lives on Work

Previously, not much has been written or formally explored regarding benefits that personal life can bring to work life. However, recent research at the Center for Creative Leadership has examined how interactions between different roles can contribute to a high-achieving woman's professional and personal development (Ruderman, Ohlott, Panzer, and King, 1999). The findings suggest that lessons learned in one aspect of life spill over into another. Six significant skills and benefits from the women's personal lives were identified as contributing to increased effectiveness at work:

1. *Interpersonal skills*—they gained experience in understanding, motivating, and respecting others

2. *Handling multiple tasks*—as a result of juggling personal tasks, setting family goals, and so forth, women were able to multitask effectively at work as well

3. *Leadership skills*—leadership opportunities in community or volunteer settings provided lessons about leadership in the workplace

4. *Psychological benefits*—feelings of self-esteem and confidence developed in the women's personal lives that helped them feel confident professionally

5. *Emotional support and advice*—getting this support from family and friends helped women succeed at work

6. *Personal interests and background*—pursuit of personal interests and cross-cultural experiences or background brought value to women's work

Often more value is placed on the learning that one does at work, but clearly lessons in personal life are valuable. The trick is to become aware of these important lessons and then capitalize on them. One executive described a complementarity of learning between herself and her husband that had implications for a more flexible leadership style at work:

> In the partnership that I have with my husband, I think we trade off on leadership roles. We balance each other very well, to the point where we have somehow adapted to and adopted some of the personality traits of one another. I've typically been more of an extrovert, my husband a little less so, but over the years I've seen the benefits of not being quite so extroverted and I think my husband has done the same in just the opposite [direction].

What in your personal life contributes to your work life?
What in your work life contributes to your personal life?

BALANCE, MASTERY, AND PARENTING

Two truly personal topics may be central to your concerns about balance. The first is the tension between mastery and intimacy. Most often this is a problem for men, but it is sometimes a problem for women also. The second is parenting, which tends to be more of a challenge for mothers but increasingly for fathers also.

Mastery Versus Intimacy

How does it happen that people who demonstrate the talent and willpower to succeed in an organization, to run multimillion-dollar operations, can be unable to run their own lives or establish a nourishing life balance? Why do these powerful, self-willed people often regard their life structure as being controlled by external forces?

Organizational values, norms, and reward systems can launch a spiral of imbalance. An executive or manager devotes increasing time and energy to work, driven by the normal rewards and expectations of work life, perhaps to gain greater recognition or to become wealthy. This produces ever greater rewards, responsibility, and pressure to work even more. Locked in this cycle, the manager increasingly neglects family or other aspects of personal life, especially if they do not provide the emotional affirmation the job does. Quite often managers deny this imbalance until a crisis explodes in their lives.

But is the organization the only source of pressure? We suggest that a leader's own needs, wants, and drives can contribute importantly to the imbalance. The lopsided allocation of time and energy may be merely a consequence, or a symptom, of deeper issues.

In *Balancing Act* (1993), based on a biographical study of senior managers, Joan Kofodimos concludes:

> Executives and managers—males in particular—tend to take a particular approach to living which we can describe as a striving for mastery and an avoidance of intimacy. *Striving for mastery* is characterized by emphasis on task accomplishment; by perception of other people as work roles, human assets, or instruments for getting the work done; and by reliance on rational analysis in making decisions. *Avoidance of intimacy* is characterized by a relative lack of empathy and compassion, inattention to our own and others' feelings, reluctance to experience and express vulnerability and self-doubt, and discomfort in being playful and spontaneous [p. 5].

Kofodimos sees organizational pressures amplifying the personal pattern. The organization encourages concentration of time and energy on work. It also rewards mastery and penalizes intimacy:

> Mastery-oriented qualities—such as ambition, confidence, power, aggressiveness, independence, and optimism—are generally seen as contributing to

a person's effectiveness. In contrast, intimacy-oriented qualities—such as asking for help, expressing feelings and doubts, being playful and sponta- neous, and demonstrating empathy and compassion—are seen as getting in the way and thus are devalued and discouraged [p. 7].

Recognizing this tension, we can more easily see how more attention is given to the workplace than to life outside of work. Although the Kofodimos study is based almost entirely on the experience and values of male executives, we suspect that women face these conflicts as well as they move increasingly into senior man- agement ranks. Consider these comments from one of our interviews:

> In the summertime, there have been times when my husband has called me
> at 8:30 or 9:00 [in the evening], saying, "Are you going to come home?" I just
> completely lose track of time because I actually enjoy what I do; I get into it
> and it's fun for me. [But] when I hear my son tell his friends that the only
> way he can reach me is to page me, then I know that I'm going overboard
> and really have to back off. That's been a hard lesson.

Do you see yourself at all in this pattern?

Do you find more rewards in accomplishing tasks?

Are there times or ways in which the mastery virtues can be counterproductive in leadership?

Are there times or ways in which the intimate virtues also serve leadership?

Parenting

When we asked managers what kinds of costs they'd paid in their careers, the typ- ical answer referred to overwork and family sacrifices. We gave several examples in Chapter Two. Here's another stressed response:

> My little inner circle for career is like nine times larger than my family life,
> and my personal life does not exist. . . . I've got to find ways to improve. . . .
> I have to have time for myself and time for my family. I feel like I'm on call
> twenty-four hours a day. Even on the weekends there is no weekend.

Another respondent had things under somewhat better control for the moment, but not without paying a price. When asked, "Right now, as an associate director, you aren't putting your sights on a particular director job or higher in the organization, for a VP slot or anything?" this manager responded:

> No. And I'll be quite honest. I am not willing to give up my family at this point. I just know what others at the vice president level need to give up. And I'm just not willing to make that sacrifice.

Much has been written and discussed about balance issues for mothers. In many but not all cases, mothers have a tougher agenda than fathers in finding a healthy life balance. For many historical, social, and psychological reasons, mothers are expected to, want to, or have to shoulder more than half the work of parenting. This makes any job or professional endeavor more problematic. A leadership role or aspirations make things even stickier.

We asked a human resource director what it meant to be a female leader in her organization. Her response: "It means that you probably have no personal life."

One of the unhappiest stories we heard came from a woman who holds an international sales position with a Fortune 500 company. The predominant culture, she said, obliged her to disguise her career-family struggles:

> I use a lot of energy trying to make it look as if I'm doing things the same as everybody else, but I'm not. My lifestyle is much different. . . . I have restrictions that I think most people don't have. It takes a lot of energy for me to cover that up, . . . or else I'm looked at as not having the flexibility, and that's exhausting. Really, the energy is [being spent] . . . to make it look as if I am doing it the traditional way when in fact I may be working at night or traveling at odd hours or dropping my son off at the airport so my husband can pick him up.

Working fathers also struggle to balance parenting and career demands, and more attention is being given to this issue. The cover story of a recent issue of *Forbes* magazine was "Dealing with Daddy Stress." "Corporate America wants them at work," the blurb said; "their families want them at home." The story featured chief executive officers acknowledging the stress that comes from expectations and responsibilities both at home and at work (Grover, 1999). There are also good books on the topic: *Working Fathers: New Strategies for Balancing Work and Family* (Levine, 1997) and *Father Courage: What Happens When Men Put Family First* (Levine, 2000) come to mind. The workplace was and still is much less accepting of the needs of fathers to attend to their personal lives, and until now this discussion has stayed pretty much undercover.

Important indicators have spelled out the dilemma for men; for example, laws and court rulings have given them job protection for family leave. But such changes haven't necessarily changed the mind-sets of the men themselves or the social expectations around them. By mid-1998, half a million men were taking parental leave each year under the auspices of the 1993 federal Family and Medical Leave Act, compared to 1.4 million women. Where were the rest of the new daddies? Some were doing their same old jobs, and others were bootlegging additional time off. James Levine, author of *Working Fathers* (1997), points out that much progress for men is "underground." Fearing that they will be labeled slackers, fathers cobble together sick days and vacation time to create leave time when a baby is born. Even years later, if they want to attend a school play, they dash for the office door under cover of attending a "late meeting."

Social forces may eventually place both sexes on a level playing field. These include the "new psychological contract" that gives less cradle-to-grave loyalty. Expectations are rising that work should become more personally fulfilling. Generation X and the one behind it (Generation Y) seem to regard organizational success as only one element in a constantly changing lifelong career that often values integration and flexibility over financial rewards. Our hope is that it will get a bit easier.

ACHIEVING BALANCE

When the important components of your life—work, family, community, health, volunteering, learning, and so forth—are reasonably aligned and mutually reinforcing, the result is a sense of comfort, confidence, strength, and well-being.

Significantly improving balance is often difficult. Solutions tend to be unique; you cannot just copy someone else's way of working things out. Your answer lies within you. You need to find within yourself something special, something that is your center of gravity—a holistic place where things come together, where the world is right for you at this point in your life. This can emerge from a combination of your competencies, values, relationships, and experiences.

Rechecking Your Values

Before reading on about five strategies for achieving balance, look back at your values exercise in Chapter Four. Note how many of the following values you rated as *always* valued and *often* valued: balance, community, family, friendship, love, physical fitness. Note where these values rated in relation to these other values: achievement, advancement, affluence, authority, status. Sometimes, in some situations, these two groups of values can be compatible, but as people take on more responsibility, the two groups may come into greater conflict.

What signs of balance or imbalance are reflected in the values exercise? How have you dealt in the past with these conflicts?

Five Strategies for Achieving Balance

There are at least five strategies for achieving balance (see Figure 6.1), and each has variations.

Integrating Integration is perhaps the most comprehensive approach. Its premise is that different needs and activities of your life should be interwoven. The idea is to identify what you really want in each area of your life and then design a life space in which you can accomplish your goals in an integrated way. At first glance, balance and integration might appear as opposites. Balance is often viewed as drawing lines between work, family, and personal life. You have contracts with yourself and with others about how much time you'll devote to these areas. When you begin to integrate, the lines become blurred. In our view, the blurring can be helpful for balance.

Figure 6.1 Strategies for Achieving Balance

- **Integrating:** Identify what you want and create a lifespace to accommodate it.

- **Narrowing:** Choose what's important, and eliminate the nonessential.

- **Moderating:** Set limits on the time and energy you give to tasks and roles.

- **Sequencing:** Set priorities—don't do everything at once.

- **Adding resources:** Get the people, systems, and money you need to take the pressure off you.

In *The Seven Habits of Highly Effective People* (1989), Stephen Covey describes a type of integrated balance for individuals (and organizations) as continual renewal along four dimensions: physical, mental, spiritual, and socioemotional: "Organizations and individuals that give recognition to each of these four dimensions in their mission statements provide a powerful framework for balance renewal" (p. 303), he writes. The idea is to set high goals in each of the four dimensions and then reach for them all. Mottoes for people adopting the integration strategy are "Go for the gold!" and "Do what you love—the money will follow." One executive endorsed integration by saying, "You're most comfortable [being] who you are all the time, rather than being one person in your personal life and another person in your employment."

The antithesis of integration is *partitioning,* creating or maintaining artificial barriers between areas of life. One interviewee described a consequent pattern and its frustrating results:

> What I tend to do is try to order my life—very, very structured. At 10:05 it's time to hug the wife. And I find myself giving up more and more spontaneity, trying to juggle these two conflicting needs. I get pretty creative: "Well, if I do this, if I schedule this meeting here and I rush over, and everything is right and I hit all the lights, then I can be at the dance recital." And so there's always tension and stress related to trying to juggle.

The integration strategy says that to isolate or rigidly compartmentalize is often counterproductive. So integration points toward easing prohibitions against things such as working at home when you could be working at the office, bringing the kids to work, making personal phone calls on company time, or connecting company-paid trips to personal vacations. Nowadays, employees and employers are knocking down these false barriers—for example, everyone seems to be "working from home" at least some if not all of the time.

This isn't to say that some partitioning isn't healthy—it is. Each element in our lives deserves our full attention at appropriate times. But the boundaries can be flexible, and opportunities for overlap can be chosen when needed. Overlapping personal and work roles can help achieve balance and flexibility. It may make sense to bring the family along on a business trip and take small excursions in the free time. We know of some women who travel with a small child and a caregiver so that they can have evenings with the child and not agonize about being away.

Integration is the theme of Sunny Hansen's book *Integrative Life Planning* (1997). Hansen challenges the traditional one-dimensional notion of career planning—matching people with jobs—because she feels that life presents the individual with so many career transitions that a single "match" won't be valid for long. She stresses the need to connect family and parenting, learning (both formal and informal), leisure, and work—meaning by work a rich, lifelong productive effort rather than any one particular job or occupational role.

Before the twentieth century (and in some cultures still today), this issue would have been irrelevant. The members of farm, artisan, and shopkeeping families worked together, and they lived where they worked. Spouses didn't need to ask at dinnertime, "So how was your day?" Kids learned directly what their parents did and how. In the twentieth century, much of the world moved away from that paradigm toward a divided life space based on commuting, office buildings, travel schedules, and relocations. Perhaps twenty-first century technology will swing the pendulum back.

Of course, integration is not without its problems. In trying to meet two needs at the same time, we may not meet both or perhaps even either of them to anyone's satisfaction. Bringing a child on a business trip may work for an executive mother, but the child, accustomed to receiving the mother's undivided attention, may not perceive this circumstance as particularly valuable or even worthwhile.

> Where do you partition your life?
>
> Which boundaries would you like to soften?
>
> What types of integration have you already tried?
>
> What has been the result?
>
> Are there any areas of your life that might become more integrated?
>
> How might this enhance your life?
>
> Have you tried a form of integration that didn't seem to benefit both sides?
>
> How might both sides be given more benefit?

Narrowing There's only so much one can do in a lifetime, and certainly only so much one can do right now. Only four cups will fit in a quart! Who among us doesn't know someone who is simply trying to do too much? Who among us hasn't felt overwhelmed by all those "nonnegotiable" top-level commitments? Narrowing the range of what's important may be the key to a better life.

Narrowing might mean simply taking a walk by yourself somewhere and deciding to offload a bunch of tasks, goals, relationships, and expectations (yours and other people's too). We all need to clean our mental closets once in a while. We do this most often at major transitions (key birthdays, relocations, promotions, and so forth) and at times of serious difficulty (severe criticism or failure, family trouble, illness). The commitments that survive the cleaning then become more important, more manageable, and easier to integrate.

Narrowing can happen at a deeper level too. Some people elect to stay single partly so that they can devote more of their life to their work. Some marry but elect not to have children. In many marriages, one partner forgoes personal ambitions and a full-time career so that the other partner can take on bigger challenges.

Choices can be made in other areas as well. It may be important to attend religious services, but that doesn't mean you have to accept the offer to be a deacon or president of the sisterhood. Perhaps it's ideal to get to the gym five days a week, but using a treadmill at home two or three days a week may have to do. A promotion to vice president of international sales might be nice, but it may not fit with everything else that's going on in your life.

One executive explained to us how he has managed to narrow commitments:

> I've tried to cut down on a lot of things in my life, try to spend time on the things that are most important to me, and consciously try to say, "Well, gee, is that really that big a deal?" If it's not, I just say no, refuse to do it, and that allows me to have enough time to do the things that are most important to me. I've always been active in a lot of different things, but I just cut back to the few that have a lot of value to me.

The narrowing strategy focuses on making only those commitments that you can keep. Doing things well may be more important than doing as much as possible. This perspective makes good common sense and is also supported by research. A study of both men and women by Donald Reitzes and Elizabeth Mutran (1994) hypothesized links between role accumulation and self-esteem. Though role accumulation alone showed no significant correlation, commitment to worker, spouse, and parent roles did correlate with increased self-esteem. In other words, selective commitments, rather than blind accumulation of roles, lead to positive outcomes.

> What are your most important commitments?
>
> What commitments do you maintain beyond their real degree of importance to you?
>
> What tasks, goals, relationships, and expectations can you offload from yourself and others in your purview?
>
> Where can you commit more fully by spreading yourself over fewer tasks?

Moderating Moderating expectations is another way of honoring commitments, especially when there isn't a choice about dropping one or another of them. You've heard the old expression: "Everything in moderation." Moderation in your life means spending the right amount of time in each area of life, not overdoing things. Does the report have to be perfect? Does the birthday party for your child have to have every bell and whistle? Do you have to take the lead on every project?

The same executive we quoted about narrowing had this to say about moderating:

> I have an agreement with my wife that I will not work later than 6:00 in the evening, and I live by that 99.9 percent of the time. I do come in [to work] early in the morning, but we're OK with that because it doesn't take away from the family. As early as I get out, I usually go to bed fairly early. But I seldom take work home. When I have a project I need to work on over the weekend—which is very, very rare—I'll come in the office early Saturday or Sunday and plug away and get home midmorning or by lunch time. Then the rest of the day is committed to the family. I think that has had a tremendous effect on the home life.

Some people harbor an unfortunate assumption about any individual who seems successful at balancing work and nonwork activities: they assume this person is not fully committed, not willing to be a dedicated member of the corporate team. Perhaps this person is even taking more from the organization than he or she is giving back—a freeloader! The fallacy of this assumption was demonstrated in the research results showing that managers and leaders who maintain good roles outside work often perform better on the job than those who maniacally work, work, work.

Your task, we suggest, is to identify and invest in the specific combination of roles that enhances your psychological well-being, your self-awareness, and your work effectiveness.

Do you have too many salient commitments?

Can some commitments be moderated?

Are your or others' expectations about you too high in some area right now?

What might be more realistic?

Sequencing This strategy says, "Yes, you can have it all (or almost all), but not all at once!" Prioritizing doesn't mean entirely giving up on options but rather doing first things first. One executive we talked with takes a seasonal perspective:

> I've always said that September and October are bad family months because I'm so busy at work. November and December are great family months because I'm not so busy at work. So the family understands what's going on.

Sequencing carries some risks. Putting something off until later may mean you'll never get to it. Many things can happen: a new stream of high priorities, illness, and so on. It's also possible that what you think is so important today will recede in importance on its own.

Many organizations start each year's budget discussion with a long wish list of new ventures, capital projects, staffing additions, and other desired goals. As they get down to discussing strategy and reality, the list gets a lot shorter. It's good to start with a long list; it's equally good to shorten it so that it can fit into one integrated effort.

Our experience in the business world suggests that about half of the dropped or cropped items eventually resurface in similar or modified form. The other half sort of disappear, mostly without great regrets. Would that be such a bad outcome?

> What work and personal goals would you put on your list of top priorities?
>
> Which few goals really require the most thought and effort now, ahead of all the others?
>
> Are there things on the list that could slide without harm?
>
> What sort of balance between work and other parts of your life results from this line of thinking?

Adding Resources A final strategy is adding resources so that more can get done. If the commitments are important, and there really isn't a good way to drop them, moderate them, or put them off until later, add resources. Here are some of the most likely ways to do so:

- Get a bigger budget.
- Add staff—permanent or temporary, perfect or otherwise—at home or at work.
- Align with people who have what you need.
- Share resources with colleagues.
- Get rid of impediments and obstacles.
- Free up underused resources.
- Hire additional services to assist with personal tasks.

Resources might include a fleet of limos or a humble rental car. They include all sorts of people. This might not only help you free up your own time but also provide benefits to others. The real question is how you use resources to help you in all areas and not just do a better job at work.

> What resources could give you better balance? Why?
>
> Which of the means cited in the text have you used recently?
>
> What other means could you be using to improve the balance in your life?

BEGINNING TO BALANCE

At this point, we'd like you to begin to draw a picture of the interactions between your world of work and your personal life. We use the leadership role question as the focal point for the other questions. How will continuing, assuming, increasing, or decreasing your leadership responsibilities fit with all of the other areas and interests in your life?

For simplicity, our questions focus on leadership at work that may be increasing in responsibility, rather than focusing on leadership in the family or in volunteer settings. But as we said in Chapter One, leadership in settings outside work is important, too, and you may be one kind of leader in one setting and another kind at work. This will be important to take into account as you move through the questions.

If the following process is leading you to decide that leadership isn't for you—or not right now, at least—that's OK. Our hope is that by asking yourself the following questions, you will gain a better perspective on your life as a whole. Each person's story and situation will be different. Skip over any questions that don't apply to you. Create your own additional questions that do reflect your story. The purpose is to reflect on how you can orient, organize, and prioritize your life interests and responsibilities to fit together in a more manageable whole. By so doing, you will be a more energized, healthy, and fulfilled person and leader.

Overview of Personal Commitments

Begin by writing down here or in your learning journal about your commitments, roles, or responsibilities outside your work.

Roles

1. List your current roles—mother, father, spouse, significant other, parent, caregiver, friend, volunteer, and so forth:

_____

_____

_____

_____

2. What's the significance of these commitments in your life?

_____

_____

_____

_____

3. On which do you spend the most time? Why?

_____

_____

_____

_____

4. On which do you spend the least time? Why?

_____

_____

_____

_____

5. Where would you like to spend more time?

_____

_____

_____

_____

6. Do you foresee changes in these roles over the next five years?

_____

_____

_____

_____

7. What will be the impact on you in terms of your needs, time, energy, and so forth?

_____

_____

_____

_____

8. How will additional leadership responsibility bring benefits to these other roles? Do other people in your life see the benefits?

_____

_____

_____

_____

9. How will additional leadership responsibility interfere with these roles? Do others agree that it will interfere?

_____

_____

_____

_____

Now look more specifically at some of your relationships and their connections to the leadership role.

Primary Relationship

1. Does your spouse or significant other appreciate and respect your attention to your role as a leader?

_____

_____

_____

_____

2. Will this person be supportive and understand the implications of additional leadership responsibility?

_____

_____

_____

_____

3. How much do you want the person involved?

_____

_____

_____

_____

4. How will you solicit his or her support?

_____

_____

_____

_____

5. Is the person also committed to a heavy organizational leadership role? If so, can the family afford both of you working at a fast pace?

_____

_____

_____

_____

6. How will the two of you share the family responsibilities?

_____

_____

_____

_____

Caretaking Roles

1. Are children, dependent parents, or other dependents living with or near you?

_____

_____

_____

_____

2. How do these relationships energize you? How do they drain your energy?

_____

_____

_____

_____

3. What kind of impact do you want to have on your family? What kind of parent do you want to be?

_____

_____

_____

_____

4. What will be the stresses for attending to these caretaking roles and your leadership role?

_____

_____

_____

_____

5. What kinds of resources can you use to help with these stresses?

_____

_____

_____

_____

6. Do you have any regrets or lessons from decisions you have made to date regarding time at work and time with family?

_____

_____

_____

_____

7. What guidelines will you use to make decisions about conflicts between work and your caretaking roles?

_____

_____

_____

_____

8. Are you thinking of starting a family? What impact will this have?

_____

_____

_____

_____

9. At what stage in life are your parents? Are they in good health? Are you their primary social support?

_____

_____

_____

_____

10. In the future, will you move closer to your parents, or they to you?

_____

_____

_____

_____

11. What type of support do you receive from your children or your parents?

_____

_____

_____

_____

12. Will they be interested in your leadership role?

_____

_____

_____

_____

Friends

1. Do you tend to have friends from your work setting or from outside your work setting?

_____

_____

_____

_____

2. What types of support do you receive from your friends?

_____

_____

_____

_____

3. How often do you get together with friends? What role do these friendships play in your life?

_____

_____

_____

_____

4. Do they express interest in your leadership role? Do you discuss it with them?

_____

_____

_____

_____

Volunteer Work

1. What type of community work do you do? What is the time commitment?

_____

_____

_____

_____

2. What benefits have you accrued from this role? What costs?

_____

_____

_____

_____

3. Could you integrate your volunteer work with both family or friend time?

_____

_____

_____

_____

4. Do you envision devoting more time to this?

_____

_____

_____

_____

After taking a thorough look at your roles, summarize in writing how your current or additional leadership responsibilities benefit you and these important relationships in your life. Also summarize the difficulties that additional leadership responsibilities will bring. Does the positive outweigh the negative?

_____

_____

_____

_____

_____

_____

Other Variables

In addition to the roles in your personal life, there are other variables to consider that affect the decisions you should and will make about leadership. Four principal variables are geographical location, your health, your age, and your financial situation.

Geographical Location

1. How important is location to you? How much did you value location in Chapter Four?

_____

_____

_____

_____

2. Do you like where you are living?

_____

_____

_____

_____

3. Do you like where you will be living if you take a new leadership role? Will there be a longer or shorter commute?

_____

_____

_____

_____

4. Would you like to live in a different climate?

_____

_____

_____

_____

5. Where is your extended family located? What weight does that carry for you?

_____

_____

_____

_____

6. Where would you like to retire?

_____

_____

_____

_____

Health

1. Is your health such that you can tolerate the long hours and stresses of your current or future leadership role?

_____

_____

_____

_____

2. What would you like to change about your health regimen in order to be up for future leadership tasks? Will you be able to fit in regular workouts with the new demands of the work?

_____

_____

_____

_____

3. How are you at taking vacations? Do you need to change the way you take vacations in order to provide more stress relief?

_____

_____

_____

_____

4. Do your various current commitments seem to prevent you from finding the energy and focus you need to seriously examine your sources of stress? How could you change that?

_____

_____

_____

_____

5. What are the incentives to keep healthy? What are the obstacles?

_____

_____

_____

_____

Age

1. How does your age affect your decisions? Do you have concerns about age?

_____

_____

_____

_____

2. What role does your age play in your leadership decisions? How many more years do you plan to work?

_____

_____

_____

_____

3. How high do you want to go in the organization?

_____

_____

_____

_____

4. When do you want to retire? How satisfied will you be with coasting until retirement?

_____

_____

_____

_____

Financial Situation

1. Will more leadership responsibilities assist you in your financial goals?

_____

_____

_____

_____

2. How much financial risk would be involved if you were to devote more time to your personal life?

_____

_____

_____

_____

3. How dependent are you on your current financial status?

_____

_____

_____

_____

To sum it all up, how do location, age, health, and personal finances bear on the possibility of more leadership responsibility for you?

_____

_____

_____

_____

_____

A CONTINUOUS PROCESS

We suggest that working to achieve balance is no easy task. Our life circumstances are constantly changing. Take a look at what Sunny Hansen (1997) reports about the amount of career change.

Citing the work of William Charland (1993), Hansen (1997) points out that each year in the United States, a third of all job roles are in transition, a third of all technical schools become obsolete, and a third of all workers leave their jobs. As a result, "part of the career professional's task is to help individuals rethink the relationship between personal transitions, their own values, and organizational social change" (p. 10). Therefore, balance also can't be static. It's a dynamic reconciliation of extremes.

As you might imagine from the description in Chapter Three, Estee Lauder's career and life presented quite a challenge to balance. The intensity of her aspirations would surely put a strain on anyone's sense of balance. She married early, and by the late 1930s, she and Joe Lauder had a son. But married life seemed to detract from her ability to put her entire self into her work, and they divorced in 1939. Not long afterward, she admitted that this was the "biggest mistake of my life." Three years later, she and Joe remarried, had another son, and stayed married—with Joe running the financial side of the company—until his death at age eighty. In her "second" marriage, Estee Lauder had found the integration of work and family that gave her the balance she needed to drive a successful business in an extremely competitive market (Koehn, 2000).

SUMMARY AND SYNTHESIS

This chapter explored the issues of balance and ways in which your roles at work and outside work affect each other. It looked at five basic strategies for achieving balance: integrating, narrowing, moderating, sequencing, and adding resources.

1. Look back over your written responses to the chapter. What forms do your balance problems take?

_____

_____

_____

_____

2. What would represent a good balance for you at this point in your life and career?

_____

_____

_____

_____

_____

3. What types of methods have you tried to achieve more balance and integration?

_____

_____

_____

_____

_____

4. Should you be trying something different?

_____

_____

_____

_____

_____

The final chapter of this book will help you synthesize the work you've completed in Chapters Two through Six. It will also help you consider the implications for future leadership decisions.

Take Steps Toward Self-Aware Leadership

By reading, reflecting on, and completing the exercises in the first six chapters, you accumulated a lot of data about yourself. This final chapter will help you synthesize this information to create a clearer picture. It will help you arrive at new insights and employ those insights in decisions about yourself and leadership. Finally, it will discuss other resources that you can seek to enhance the process. We hope that the chapter will help you clarify your decision making about leadership. Consider the process an ongoing one: continue to add and use new relevant data—facts, insights, feedback, emerging patterns, career options, and so forth.

SUMMARIZING THE RELEVANT FACTS

Figures 7.1 and 7.2 are tools to help you summarize your main conclusions from earlier chapters. Figure 7.1 places various topics from the chapters in the conceptual framework that we introduced in Chapter One. Figure 7.2 is a blank version in which you can write the salient ideas that you collected about yourself. (You may want to photocopy and enlarge Figure 7.2 each time you wish to use it.)

In Figure 7.2, write down words or phrases from the exercises that hold particular meaning for you. For example, for the outer rim, what realities or external expectations set the context for your work and personal life? For the vision sector, what key words or phrases capture your personal and leadership visions? For the values sector, what values and conflicts emerge most strongly? Continue around the wheel, revisiting the contents of each chapter.

After filling in the entire wheel, study the results. What relationships do you see among your phrases in the five sectors of the framework? Do you see connections between different items within each sector? For example, do you see a connection between your main view of leadership (Chapter Two) and your leadership competencies (Chapter Five)? Your core values (Chapter Four) and role models (Chapter Three)? What insights come from looking at the entire wheel? Do you like the picture you see? Is the leadership role you are currently in or seeking likely to reflect and support all of these dimensions in your life? What is missing?

If you find that things are missing, you might want to take another blank wheel and create a future picture. Pick a future point in time (say, three years), and write the words that convey where you want to be by then. What new competencies do you wish to gain? Do you anticipate taking on a new role (such as parenting) that

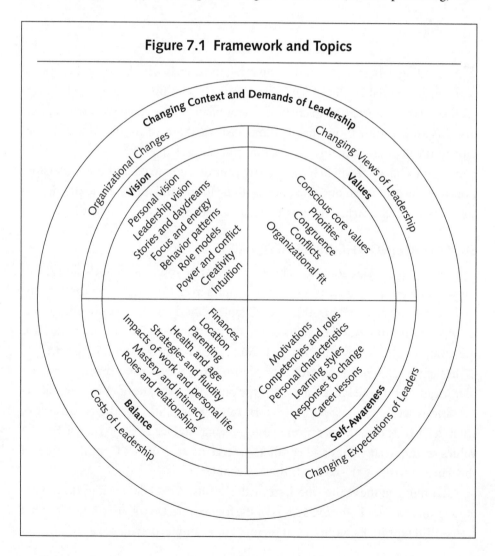

Figure 7.1 Framework and Topics

would change the picture significantly? Do you anticipate the organizational context changing a great deal? What will it look like?

FINDING PATTERNS AND LABELING THEMES

Continue by looking for broad patterns and themes that are reflected in your wheel. The themes should encapsulate major concerns, needs, or drives related to leadership and its place in your life.

You should be able to write a number of themes. For example, suppose that you observe the following pattern: a service motivation to lead, a view of leadership as

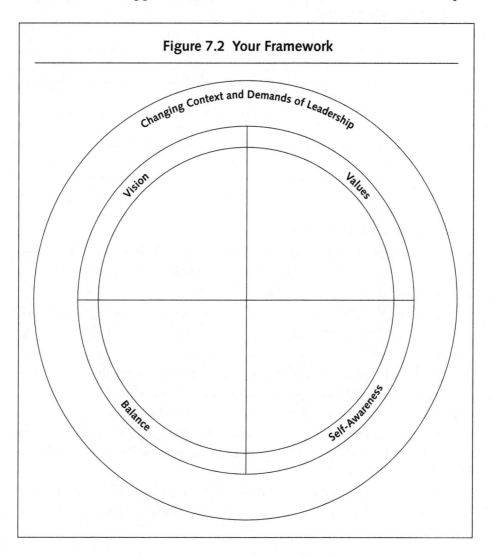

Figure 7.2 Your Framework

Changing Context and Demands of Leadership

Vision

Values

Balance

Self-Awareness

a calling, a vision of starting a new program for underprivileged children, and primary leadership roles as nurturer and facilitator. From that pattern you might abstract a leadership theme of "giving to others."

Or suppose that you found creating strategic vision to be one of your competencies, farsightedness a personal trait, achievement and recognition primary values, and entrepreneurship one of your passions; from that pattern you might cull a theme that you would label "desire for independence with impact."

Continue to look for patterns throughout the wheel; generate as many themes as you can, and label each one with a meaningful phrase.

What themes do you see?

_____

_____

_____

_____

_____

CHOOSING BELL RINGERS

The next step is to arrive at one or more "bell ringers." Bell ringers are insights that you accept as major truths about yourself—the kinds of truths or facts that can serve as lights for guidance into the future.

Test each of your themes to see whether it contains one or more potential bell ringers. For the first example we mentioned, giving to others, a bell ringer might be "I won't be totally satisfied in a leadership role unless I am doing things for other people." The bell ringer for the second example, independence with impact, could be "I need to find a role within or outside the organization where I can use my entrepreneurial talents in a way that will have a widespread impact on the industry."

A bell ringer can be an anchor. To yourself and the world it says, "Here's where I stand. This is what really matters to me. Everything else will find its place in my life if this anchor is set."

A bell ringer can also be a navigational aid. It may serve as a polestar, allowing you to zig and zag through the mazes of life, always knowing which way is forward.

"California or Bust" read the signs on horse-drawn wagons in the gold rush of 1849. Your bell ringer can say, "That's where I'm going, folks. That's where I plan to end up."

We hope that after reviewing your data, themes, and patterns, you will find one or two statements worthy of being called bell ringers. They may confirm familiar self-knowledge, or they may be epiphanies, new discoveries of who you are. Here are more examples:

> "I've been assuming leadership roles almost all my life! There's no way I can—or would want to—stop doing it now."

> "What turns me on is being in the spotlight and getting the credit. Perhaps I shouldn't revel in these things, but I do. It'll be better for me to accept this part of me and make my decisions accordingly."

> "I just can't sit back when there is leadership work to be done. It drives me crazy to see things in a mess, and it is rewarding to get them organized. That's how I am, and that's how I'll always be."

> "I need my privacy. If leadership means living in a fishbowl, then I say, 'Forget it!'"

> "My family need me now, and I need them. Organizational leadership will either have to wait or else accommodate to my family's needs."

> "I love my professional work. I do it really well. That's how I want to spend my life—doing high-quality technical work. I'll help with some of the administrative stuff, but I don't want the top job."

> "I just can't work for someone else. I don't take orders well, especially from people I don't respect or from well-meaning boards and committees. I'll work on my own, thank you."

> "I have 'social service' written all over me. I don't feel good about myself unless I'm helping people—especially kids—with some of my leadership time and energy."

A bell ringer must be something that is really important to you; only one or perhaps two other facts, themes, or patterns might be of equal importance. It must truly "ring your bell." It needs to be something that you can tell your spouse, parents, or best friends, and they'll know that you're right. On and around such an insight you can make decisions about leadership and other things as well.

If you don't find one or two bell ringers, don't lose heart. Not everyone has one, nor is it necessary that you have one now or ever. However, if one is there, it's essential that you identify it.

Look back over your themes. Look again at facts and patterns that emerged from the earlier chapters. Write some bell ringers.

1. _____

_____

_____

2. _____

_____

_____

3. _____

_____

_____

WEIGHING COSTS AND BENEFITS

In Chapter Two, we discussed some costs of leadership. Elsewhere in the book, we highlighted possible rewards or benefits. In this concluding chapter, you can now weigh the costs and rewards of leadership. As part of the following work, you may want to revisit your recorded comments from Chapters Two and Five, where most of the rewards are mentioned.

Figure 7.3 summarizes some costs that you may want to consider. It also lists some possible benefits. Of course, one person's costs may be another person's benefits.

Among the leaders with whom we have dealt, the two most central rewards of leadership are the financial payoffs and pride of accomplishment.

Financial payoffs are both acknowledgments of short-term performance and incentives for long-term loyalty. Money also serves as a personal measure of success. It's the easiest and most common answer to the question "How am I doing?"

Money can measure year-to-year progress and permits you to compare your success with that of others in your department, company, profession, or family.

But consider that you might just as easily make the same money (or more) outside leadership, as a successful professional or entrepreneur; and financial rewards are not what people look back on when they assess their success in life, no matter how large money looms in the early stages of their careers.

By pride of accomplishment we mean mainly pride in one's impact on events or other people. Most people point with pride to successes they helped achieve.

Figure 7.3 Possible Costs and Benefits of Leadership

Costs	Benefits
Physical energy	Pride of accomplishment
Long hours	Financial rewards
Too many meetings	Self-validation
Constant obligations	Impact on people and events
Responsibility	Service to others
Caretaking	Meaning
Less time for nonleadership work interests	Attention and recognition
	Personal prominence
Visibility ("fishbowl")	New connections and acquaintances
Public duties	Helping others grow
Isolation from peers	Perquisites of office
Less freedom of expression	More resources for family
Pressure to produce	Personal status
Stress on family	Singular achievements
Less time for family	Heightened experience
Less time for other pursuits	More autonomy
Emotional strains	Travel linked to recreation
Very little feedback	Good relocations
Less useful feedback	Change
Too much travel	Control
Bad relocations	Respect
Job insecurity	Inclusion

Leadership roles aren't the only way to make that happen, but your accomplishments can be larger if you leverage the efforts of other people.

On a grand scale, buildings, streets, or even whole towns often carry a leader's name—think of Hershey, Pennsylvania, and Levittown, New York. But don't forget that Roebling was just as proud of his Brooklyn Bridge as Eiffel was of his tower. More modestly, some leaders point to a product they invented or helped produce or a successful advertising campaign that took great time and effort. You might find your greatest pride in something as "ordinary" as managing a champion Little League team or as unusual as having liberated a neighborhood from drugs and violence. If you were there in a leadership role, you had an impact on events. You helped make something happen.

Use Figure 7.3 and additional thoughts to build your own comparative list of the five or six most important costs and benefits.

Costs	Benefits
_____	_____
_____	_____
_____	_____
_____	_____
_____	_____

Overall, for you, do the benefits of holding a leadership position outweigh the costs? The number of items in each column will not determine whether costs outweigh benefits or vice versa. You will need to compare the lists and assign a level of importance to each item to determine which way the scale leans. Write your reactions to your cost-benefit list here.

_____

_____

_____

_____

If the current balance isn't rewarding, are there changes in your role or leadership setting that could tip the scales in favor of the benefits?

_____

_____

_____

_____

_____

_____

THE LEADERSHIP DECISION LADDER

Early in this book, we argued that people should assume leadership positions by conscious choice, not by default. We also stressed that the developmental process of growing in leadership should be based on a clear understanding of yourself as a person and what leadership can mean to you.

Having done the summary and thematic work suggested in the preceding sections, you may be ready now to exercise more conscious choices about yourself as a leader in current and possibly future positions in your current organization, a different organization, or some other sphere of your life. Now might be a good time to see where you are in your decision-making process.

Figure 7.4 provides a sequence and a metaphor for thinking about the stages in your next overall leadership decision. The "decision ladder" in the figure has five rungs, each representing a decision and an accomplishment in itself. To say that you are standing on a certain rung will imply that you've already climbed up more or less comfortably from the rungs below. It also suggests that your next task is to reach for the next rung. We suspect that you will be happiest with yourself if you are either moving up the ladder in a relatively concerted way or can make a conscious decision to postpone further leadership commitments. Of course, you can also always leave the ladder in order to pursue some other more compelling vision in your life and work.

In your decision-making process, the ultimate goal is to answer the question on the highest rung. Use the following descriptions and questions to determine your position on the ladder.

Rung 1: Who are you as a leader? This represents basic self-knowledge about personal vision, values, competencies, and so forth, that you have generated in this book. Who are you or might you be as a leader?

_____

_____

_____

_____

_____

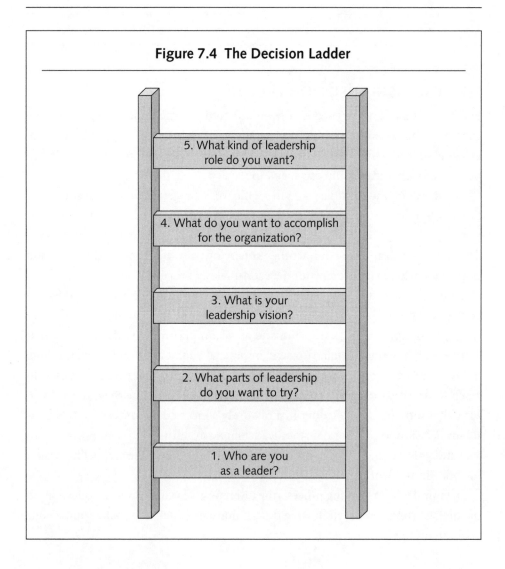

Figure 7.4 The Decision Ladder

5. What kind of leadership role do you want?

4. What do you want to accomplish for the organization?

3. What is your leadership vision?

2. What parts of leadership do you want to try?

1. Who are you as a leader?

Rung 2: What parts of leadership do you want to try? This rung provides for the fact that many decisions deal with "trying it out" or "learning what's involved" or "seeing if I'm any good" or "if I like it." Leadership is a complex and very personal experience, one not adequately understood until it is experienced firsthand. Also, leadership experiences differ, depending on the situation or organization. Have you become clearer about what you'd like to try or learn about leadership?

_____

_____

_____

_____

Rung 3: What is your leadership vision? This is the message or vision that you possess that can serve as a basis for where you want to go with leadership. Think in personal terms about what you have to say or want to express about yourself. Is there something about yourself that you feel is worth building on and making known? Do you have something to offer the world—perhaps a skill, a message, or even a dream?

_____

_____

_____

_____

Rung 4: What do you want to accomplish for the organization? What do you want to achieve in an organizational sense? How do you intend to advance the organization? Try to express your goal as a sharply defined personal or organizational target, outcome, or objective. Look back at your bell ringers: do they suggest what you want to make happen for others?

_____

_____

_____

_____

Rung 5: What kind of leadership role do you want? Note what you've said previously about what you want to become, express, learn, and achieve as a leader. What does all that say about a leadership role for you? Can you decide something about the proper place for leadership in your life at this time, in light of the options available to you? Is there a need to make an important decision at this time, or should you make a temporizing kind of decision? How much is really clear to you at this point? Keep in mind that your decision may be a short-term one, a decision on how to use a part of your time, or a long-term commitment.

_____

_____

_____

_____

_____

On the fifth rung, also consider the leadership opportunities available to you. How might these leadership roles help you accomplish your personal vision? Does your current leadership role fit into your leadership and personal visions? What future opportunities do you see that will help you get there?

_____

_____

_____

_____

_____

Where are you now on the decision ladder?

What's the next rung up?

Do you want to move up?

Are you nearly ready to do so?

What additional information or other resources will you need to climb to the next rung?

What will it take for you to move up?

NEXT STEPS

What's next? Perhaps you have had some insights as a result of your personal assessment in this book that have led you to redefine where and how you want to lead. Perhaps you will file this information away for another time. Whatever you decide, we have several suggestions:

- Let your decisions rest at least overnight before announcing anything to the world. Your words may look different to you in the morning.

- After the rest, share your decisions with friends who serve as sounding boards and trusted sources of feedback for you. Confirmations are welcome; disconfirmations are important!

- Even at that point, you may want to hold your tentative decisions for a few days, a week, or perhaps a bit longer.

See how the decisions feel as you let them seep into your identity and dreams. If they hold up well and feel even better, they are probably on target.

Once you make a decision, it is important to begin focusing on the steps or goals that will help you implement that decision. We assume that as a person in a formal role within an organization, you know a lot about setting goals and are familiar with various techniques. You know that goals must be specific and measurable. They need to be supported by target completion dates, whatever resources may be required, and a means of measuring progress. Now, or at some point in the near future, try answering the following questions.

> What are the goals that would enable you to implement this decision?
>
> How much does each goal interest you?
>
> What specific activities serve the goals?
>
> What are appropriate timelines for completion?
>
> Whose support will you need to solicit?
>
> What other resources may you need?
>
> Can you find support both within and outside of the organization?
>
> What will be the benefits to you?
>
> Will there be benefits to others?
>
> How will you hold yourself accountable?

It's also important to be realistic about your goals. Some activities may be easy to accomplish. But inevitably, if you are making a large and tough decision, there are always obstacles and distractions, including other intriguing opportunities, lack of time, unexpected changes, low motivation, and lack of support from others. To foresee both supportive forces and barriers, look back at your history regarding goals.

In the past, what has prevented you from accomplishing goals?

In the past, what methods or resources have enabled you to accomplish your goals?

What can you do to overcome the barriers?

How can you build in more support?

GETTING THE HELP YOU NEED

Appendix B contains lists of useful books, articles, and self-assessment instruments that can help you further explore what leadership might mean for you.

Also use other people as resources, so that you don't travel this journey alone. When we discussed this book with colleagues, many said things such as, "People would benefit from coaching while pursuing this framework." "Keep them aware of informal networks." "Keep your readers in touch with support. They shouldn't just muddle through." "A career counselor might be helpful in sorting out the issues." In keeping with this good advice, seek mentoring, coaching, and candid feedback from others.

Feedback is a valuable commodity for any executive. It can offer insights into your behaviors and thoughts. It can let you know how you are doing in your everyday work and how you are affecting others. It can help you stay aware of how the changes you seek for yourself may appear either helpful or disruptive to other members of your family or organization. Feedback can also help you evaluate things in the face of a setback or opportunity. As you continue to use the framework of this book, others can prod you, poke you, tell you the truth, and reveal their perceptions of you.

Because no one learns or grows in a vacuum, developmental relationships can be good sources of feedback and other support. There is no prototypical developmental relationship, no one role or combination of roles that has to be present in order to make it "developmental." Seek out multiple relationships for development. Once your needs have been clarified, the question becomes "Who can best meet these needs?" It is unlikely that one person can do it all for you. Find the right coach for the need at hand.

Use lateral, subordinate, or external relationships. An experienced colleague, a peer in another division, or even the retired executive who lives down the street may serve your developmental needs. Developmental relationships need not be long-term or intense. The question is simply whether the relationship brings a different perspective, provides new knowledge, sustains your willingness to engage and confidence in your capabilities, or keeps you motivated.

Cynthia McCauley and Christina Douglas (1998) distinguish different types of developmental relationships. Let's look at several that we think are particularly appropriate for decisions regarding the choice to lead. You shouldn't need a committee to cover them. You may find that they all reside in two or three people you happen to know.

Sounding Board

One of the first people you might want is someone with whom to discuss your internal satisfactions and dissatisfactions about your leadership role. The person may be helpful simply by standing by as you think aloud about vision, values, self-awareness, and other aspects of yourself. Or you might ask this person questions like this: "I know something about my values, but what have you noticed that I haven't picked up about myself in this area?" "Do I seem sufficiently motivated to you? What makes you think so?"

The sounding board can be a peer, colleague, spouse, friend, acquaintance—even the guy or gal who's always at the local club on Wednesday nights. The important thing is that the relationship be consistent and that the person be willing to hear you out. When choosing someone for the role, McCauley and Douglas (1998) suggest asking, "Who is good at thinking out loud and considering alternatives? Who am I willing to share my uncertainties with?" (p. 170).

Counselor

A counselor can encourage you to explore the emotional aspects of the personal work you are doing. He or she can also help you vent and express your frustrations and negative emotions without feeling judged.

For instance, you may have some doubts about your capacity to develop and sustain a personal vision. Perhaps you have always felt uncomfortable operating on that level; you've left the pie-in-the-sky stuff to others. But now we've asked you to express your vision and assured you that you have one. Now you must surface it, name it, and look at it from different angles.

A counselor can be both an objective party and someone to fall back on when the going gets tough. In choosing a counselor, you might ask, "Will she be my confidante as I struggle with this goal?" "Is he both emphatic and objective?" "Does she understand me enough to see through my excuses and procrastination?" (McCauley and Douglas, 1998, p. 171).

Cheerleader

Not only are they fun to be around, but cheerleaders can provide a valuable service for anyone trying to grow. These people are great at offering support, encouragement, and affirmation. They cheer you on as you progress. They take you out to dinner when you discover your vision or take you on a fishing trip as a reward for having figured out your leadership profile.

When looking for cheerleaders, ask questions like these: "Who is always able to make me feel competent?" "With whom can I share my small successes?" "Who is in a position to reward my successes?" (McCauley and Douglas, 1998, p. 171).

Cohort

Perhaps you know people who are also engaged in learning about themselves as leaders. These are the folks you want to talk with, if they're willing, about your respective development progress, how each of you got to this point, and where each of you plans to go from here. You can garner comfort from the struggles and the successes of your cohorts, and you will not feel all alone.

Ask questions like these when considering cohorts: "Who would understand what I am going through?" "Who are my peers in this situation?" "Who is also taking this journey and would be good company on the way?" (McCauley and Douglas, 1998, p. 171).

Mentor

Mentoring is a helping role that some executives assume. It is institutionalized in many organizations. There may be a senior person in your organization who has already been through a process similar to the one that you are now undergoing. In a more or less official mentoring role, he or she can provide an organizational perspective, linking your developmental quest to the larger management development strategy, to business strategies, and to personnel practices.

Or there may be someone else in your field but outside your organization who has had experiences like your own and is particularly interested in helping you define yourself as a leader. This person can act as a mentor for you while you are going through the process. One leader we interviewed described an important mentoring relationship:

> One of the people I consider a mentor . . . is a consultant who was here [to work with me]. In my mind, he's an incredible leader. He let me know if I was off track and not concentrating on the things I should be. He was able to assist me in problems I'd never faced before, due to my lack of experience. He was like my coach. I made a lot more improvement on the leadership side in the twelve months with him than I learned in my twelve years prior to that.

When considering someone to become your mentor, you might ask, "Does he or she have the time, motivation, and experience to help me through this?"

SUMMARY AND SYNTHESIS

Understanding how leadership plays across your life can be a messy process of difficult lessons and sometimes astonishing serendipity. There is no single switch that turns on the lights, no single fix for what may be broken. In the final analysis, vision, values, perspectives, and roles, even if examined apart, must be integrated. Concepts merge and shift. Ideas from one realm feed ideas in others. There is no one starting point, no finish-line tape, no starting gun except the one you fire.

Success at leadership is a lifelong task, a perpetual self-examination. Rewards can change. Tasks are defined by their contexts—who is involved, what else is happening, and what needs to happen. Your own goals change as time passes. Each context and each new goal requires a somewhat different use of your resources.

The process of making yourself more complete as a leader is driven by your evolving life story. All definitions and concepts are forged on the anvil of that story, that vision. If there are no passions, no dreams, no reason to make things happen involving other people, then there is little reason to add leadership to your life. If the passions are there, then the choice can still be either to hitch your wagon to the star of someone else who shares those passions or to assume the burdens and privileges of leadership yourself.

Your willingness to test your personal hypotheses, to plant a stake, to learn, and to go forward has brought you into a learning loop. With the help of peers, mentors, coaches, and honest feedback, you can move through a developmental sequence with focus, guidance, and encouragement. Stay conscious of where you want to go. Keep moving, and enjoy your journey.

Who are you? Who do you want to be? How would you like the story of your life to continue? What are you tempted to write on these lines about your future as a leader?

_____

_____

_____

_____

_____

_____

_____

_____

_____

_____

_____

_____

_____

APPENDIX A:
PROGRAM PARTICIPANT QUESTIONNAIRE

The following interview questions were asked of thirty-two Center for Creative Leadership program participants. The questions were developed to ascertain participants' current leadership roles, their visions for themselves, their values, and aspects of their personal lives. The purpose of these interviews was to learn what these leaders thought about how leadership fit into their lives and careers.

1. You have learned a lot about yourself this week—as a person and as a leader. Describe how you see leadership fitting into your life.

2. What is your philosophy of leadership?

3. How would you describe your current leadership role?

4. Was your pursuit of a leadership role a conscious decision?

5. Do you have a vision for yourself as a leader?

6. Describe how you have made some decisions about your career.

7. What kind of impact do you hope to make with your leadership? Why?

8. Describe an experience or event in which your leadership made a difference.

9. Describe a leadership experience in which your values were most prominent.

10. Describe a leadership experience in which you experienced a values conflict.

11. What are the rewards of leading?

12. What are the risks of leading?

13. What costs or sacrifices do you incur from being in a leadership role?

14. Do you see yourself in a leadership role outside work? How does this benefit you at work?

15. How does your organizational leadership role positively influence the other areas of your life?

16. How does your organizational leadership role detract from the other areas of your life?

17. Are there any specific lessons you want to pursue? How will a leadership role help you do that?

18. What kind of leadership opportunity do you see yourself pursuing in the future?

APPENDIX B: LEADERSHIP RESOURCES

We provide here a list of books and articles and descriptions of self-assessments that can be helpful in your personal journey.

BOOKS AND ARTICLES

Ambrose, D. *Leadership: The Journey Inward.* Dubuque, Iowa: Kendall/Hunt, 1991.

Autry, J. A. *Life and Work: A Manager's Search for Meaning.* New York: Morrow, 1994.

Badaracco, J. L., Jr. *Leadership and the Quest for Integrity.* Boston: Harvard Business School Press, 1989.

Bennis, W. G., and Goldsmith, J. *Learning to Lead: A Workbook on Becoming a Leader.* Reading, Mass.: Addison-Wesley, 1994.

Bolman, L. G., and Deal, T. E. *Leading with Soul: An Uncommon Journey of Spirit.* San Francisco: Jossey-Bass, 1994.

Cashman, K. *Leadership from the Inside Out: Becoming a Leader for Life.* Provo, Utah: Executive Excellence, 1998.

Ciulla, J. B. "Leadership Ethics: Mapping the Territory." *Business Ethics Quarterly,* 1995, *5*(1), 5–28.

Conger, J. A. "Personal Growth Training: Snake Oil or Pathway to Leadership?" *Organizational Dynamics,* 1994, *22*(1), 19–30.

Covey, S. R. *Principle-Centered Leadership.* New York: Summit Books, 1991.

Daudelin, M. W. "Learning from Experience Through Reflection." *Organizational Dynamics,* 1996, *24*(3), 36–48.

Dreher, D. *The Tao of Personal Leadership.* New York: HarperBusiness, 1996.

Drucker, P. F. "Managing Oneself." *Harvard Business Review,* 1999, *77*(2), 66–74.

Fairholm, G. W. *Values Leadership: Toward a New Philosophy of Leadership.* New York: Praeger, 1991.

Francis, D., and Woodcock, M. *Unblocking Organizational Values.* Glenview, Ill.: Scott, Foresman, 1990.

Fritz, S. M., Brown, F. W., Lunde, J. P., and Banset, E. A. (eds.). *Interpersonal Skills for Leadership.* Needham Heights, Mass.: Allyn & Bacon, 1996.

Hagberg, J. O. *Real Power: Stages of Personal Power in Organizations.* (rev. ed.) Salem, Wis.: Sheffield, 1994.

Handy, C. B. *The Hungry Spirit: Beyond Capitalism: A Quest for Purpose in the Modern World.* New York: Broadway Books, 1998.

Hendricks, G., and Ludeman, K. *The Corporate Mystic: A Guidebook for Visionaries with Their Feet on the Ground.* New York: Bantam Books, 1996.

Hickman, C. R. *Mind of a Manager, Soul of a Leader.* New York: Wiley, 1990.

Hillman, J. *Kinds of Power: A Guide to Its Intelligent Uses.* New York: Currency, 1995.

Hitt, W. D. *Ethics and Leadership: Putting Theory into Practice.* Columbus, Ohio: Battelle, 1990.

Hitt, W. D. *A Global Ethic: The Leadership Challenge.* Columbus, Ohio: Battelle, 1996.

Hosmer, L. T. *Moral Leadership in Business.* Burr Ridge, Ill.: Irwin, 1994.

Jones, L. B. *The Path: Creating Your Mission Statement.* New York: Hyperion, 1996.

Kerr, S. (ed.). *Ultimate Rewards: What Really Motivates People to Achieve.* Boston: Harvard Business School Press, 1997.

Kidder, R. M. *How Good People Make Tough Choices.* New York: Morrow, 1995.

Koehn, N. F. "Estee Lauder: Self-Definition and the Modern Cosmetics Market." In P. Scranton (ed.), *Beauty and Business.* New York: Routledge, 2000.

Kuczmarski, S. S., and Kuczmarski, T. D. *Values-Based Leadership.* Upper Saddle River, N.J.: Prentice Hall, 1995.

Kummerow, J. M., Barger, N. J., and Kirby, L. K. *Worktypes: Understand Your Work Personality—How It Helps You and Holds You Back, and What You Can Do to Understand It.* New York: Warner Books, 1997.

Lessem, R. *Developmental Management: Principles of Holistic Business.* Cambridge, Mass.: Blackwell, 1990.

Levine, J. *Working Fathers: New Strategies for Balancing Work and Family.* Reading, Mass.: Addison-Wesley, 1997.

McCauley, C. D., and Douglas, C. A. "Developmental Relationships." In C. D. McCauley, R. Moxley, and E. Van Velsor (eds.), *The Center for Creative Leadership Handbook of Leadership Development.* San Francisco: Jossey-Bass, 1998.

McKenna, E. P. *When Work Doesn't Work Anymore.* New York: Delacorte Press, 1997.

Morgan, S., and Dennehy, R. F. "The Power of Organizational Storytelling: A Management Development Perspective." *Journal of Management Development,* 1997, *16*(7), 494–501.

Moxley, R. *Leadership and Spirit: Breathing New Vitality and Energy into Individuals and Organizations.* San Francisco: Jossey-Bass, 1999.

Palus, C. J., Nasby, W., and Easton, R. D. *Understanding Executive Performance: A Life-Story Perspective.* Greensboro, N.C.: Center for Creative Leadership, 1991.

Pearson, C. S. *The Hero Within: Six Archetypes We Live By.* (3rd ed.) San Francisco: HarperSanFrancisco, 1998.

Petrick, J. A., and Quinn, J. F. *Management Ethics: Integrity at Work.* Thousand Oaks, Calif.: Sage, 1997.

Pfeffer, J. "Understanding Power in Organizations." *California Management Review,* Winter 1992, pp. 29–50.

Pulley, M. L. *Losing Your Job, Reclaiming Your Soul.* San Francisco: Jossey-Bass, 1997.

Quigley, J. V. *Vision: How Leaders Develop It, Share It, and Sustain It.* New York: McGraw-Hill, 1994.

Rosener, J. "Ways Women Lead." *Harvard Business Review,* 1990, *68*(6), 119–125.

Shelton, K. *Beyond Counterfeit Leadership: How You Can Become a More Authentic Leader.* Provo, Utah: Executive Excellence, 1997.

Sherman, S. "Leaders Learn to Heed the Voice Within." *Fortune,* Aug. 24, 1994, pp. 92–100.

Shipka, B. *Leadership in a Challenging World: A Sacred Journey.* Boston: Butterworth-Heinemann, 1997.

Simmons, S., and Simmons, J. C. *Measuring Emotional Intelligence: The Groundbreaking Guide to Applying the Principles of Emotional Intelligence.* Arlington, Tex.: Summit Publishing Group, 1997.

Wentling, R. M. "Women in Management: A Longitudinal Study of Their Career Development and Aspirations." *A Leadership Journal: Women in Leadership—Sharing the Vision,* 1997, *2*(1), 93–107.

Zaleznik, A. *Learning Leadership: Cases and Commentaries on Abuses of Power in Organizations.* Chicago: Bonus Books, 1993.

SELF-ASSESSMENTS

The following instruments can be self-administered and self-scored or administered with very little supervision. The descriptions and phone numbers were taken from M. K. Schwartz, K. M. Axtman, and F. H. Freeman (eds.), *Leadership Resources: A Guide to Training and Development Tools* (7th ed.), Greensboro, N.C.: Center for Creative Leadership, 1998. Please refer to that volume for more information on these instruments.

Change Agent Questionnaire

This instrument measures personal philosophy about change and one's strategies for effecting change. It contains forty-five alternative sets of attitudes to be ranked on a 10-point scale. When participants complete their grids, they learn about their one dominant and four backup styles of change orientation. This instrument is available from Teleometrics International, (800) 527-0406.

The Comprehensive Leader: A New View of Visionary Leadership

The authors' premise is that at the heart of leadership is knowledge—about oneself, others, one's organization, and the world. Visionary leadership develops comprehensive knowledge and builds a future based on that knowledge. These two behaviors and four levels of knowledge are assessed in this 360-degree inventory. The participant responds to how well his or her behaviors match forty statements of knowledge-based behavior. Other observers who know the participant provide feedback on the same forty items to create a comprehensive leadership profile. Available from HRDQ, (800) 633-4533.

Executive Profile Survey

This test is based on ten years of research to identify empirically the major self-attitudes, self-beliefs, and values patterns shared by executives. Eleven scales reflect the core of the occupational self-concept of two thousand top-level executives, including bank presidents, Fortune 500 CEOs, newspaper editors, and college presidents. The scales are ambition, assertiveness, enthusiasm, creativity, spontaneity, self-reliance, consideration, flexibility, emotional control, practicality, and efficiency. Available from IPAT, (800) 225-4728.

Insight Inventory

Individuals respond to thirty-two adjectives to describe their behavior at work and again to describe their behavior outside work. The scores reveal a profile of how individuals get their own way (direct or indirect), respond to people (reserved or outgoing), pace activities (urgent or steady), and deal with details (unstructured or precise). Available from HRD Press, (800) 822-2801.

Leadership/Personality Compatibility Inventory (L/PCI)

This inventory is designed to help managers understand how the compatibility between basic personality style and leadership role may affect leadership effectiveness. A personality inventory measures four dominant personality types: bold, express, sympathetic, or technical. A leadership role inventory measures leadership characteristics: active/competitive, persuasive/interactive, precise/systematic, and willing/steady. Available from Associated Consultants in Education, (415) 492-9190.

Life Styles Inventory

This instrument was developed to assist individuals in identifying and understanding their thinking patterns and self-concept. The twelve scales (thinking styles) that make up the instrument are humanistic-encouraging, affiliative, approval, conventional, dependent, avoidance, oppositional, power, competitive, perfectionistic, achievement, and self-actualization. Available from Human Synergistics, Inc., (800) 622-7584.

Managerial Work-Values Scale

Measuring managers' work values, this instrument focuses on nine values: creativity, economics, independence, status, service, academics, security, collegiality, and work conditions. A paired-comparison format is used to establish the relative strengths of the values for the individual. May be copied from J. W. Pfeiffer, *The 1991 Annual: Developing Human Resources* (pp. 163–177), San Francisco: Jossey-Bass & Pfeiffer, 1991.

Personal Profile System

This instrument provides a framework for understanding human behavior in general and an individual's behavior specifically. Individuals make selections in twenty-eight sets of adjectives that describe their most and least characteristic behaviors. When the scores are charted and interpreted, individuals learn about their tendencies for dominance, influence, conscientiousness, and steadiness. Available from Carlson Learning Company, (800) 657-2235.

Power Base Inventory

The PBI measures the following managerial power styles: information giving, expertise, goodwill, authority, reward, and discipline. Power is defined as the ability to influence people, either through personal power or position power. Individuals select whichever of a pair of statements is more descriptive of the reasons why subordinates might comply with their wishes or beliefs. Available from Consulting Psychologists Press, (800) 624-1765.

Strength Deployment Inventory

This inventory measures an individual's self-reported style of relating to others under two conditions: when things are going well and when things are not going well and the respondent is in conflict with others. Scores are plotted on an "interpersonal interaction triangle" and graphically illustrate the individual's strength of motivation toward four polarities: altruistic-nurturing, assertive-directing, analytic-autonomizing, and flexible-cohering. Available from Personal Strengths Publishing, Inc., (800) 624-7347.

REFERENCES

Arts & Entertainment Network. "Estee Lauder." *Biography,* June 7, 1999.

Bennis, W. G., and Nanus, B. *Leaders: The Strategies for Taking Charge.* New York: HarperCollins, 1985.

Brown, T. "Leadership: A Personal Journey." *Leader to Leader,* Summer 1998, pp. 7–9.

Bunker, K. A. "The 'R' Factor in Downsizing." *Issues & Observations,* 1994, *14*(4), 8–9.

Cameron, J. *The Artist's Way: A Spiritual Path to Higher Creativity.* Los Angeles: Tarcher/Perigee, 1992.

Campbell, D. *Campbell Leadership Index (CLI).* Rosemont, Ill.: NCS Workforce Development, 1998.

Cashman, K. *Leadership from the Inside Out: Becoming a Leader for Life.* Provo, Utah: Executive Excellence, 1998.

Charland, W. *Career Shifting: Starting Over in a Changing Economy.* Holbrook, Mass.: Adams, 1993.

Cohen, B., and Greenfield, J. *Ben and Jerry's Double Dip: Lead with Your Values and Make Money, Too.* New York: Simon & Schuster, 1997.

Conger, J. A. "How Generational Shifts Will Transform Organizational Life." In F. Hesselbein, M. Goldsmith, and R. Beckhard (eds.), *The Organization of the Future.* San Francisco: Jossey-Bass, 1997.

Covey, S. R. *The Seven Habits of Highly Effective People.* New York: Simon & Schuster, 1989.

Dalton, M. A. *Becoming a More Versatile Learner.* Greensboro, N.C.: Center for Creative Leadership, 1998.

Drath, W. H., and Palus, C. J. *Making Common Sense: Leadership as Meaning-Making in a Community of Practice.* Greensboro, N.C.: Center for Creative Leadership, 1994.

Drucker, P. F. "Introduction: Toward the New Organization." In F. Hesselbein, M. Goldsmith, and R. Beckhard (eds.), *The Organization of the Future.* San Francisco: Jossey-Bass, 1997.

Drucker, P. F. *Managing in a Time of Great Change.* New York: Truman Talley/Dutton, 1995.

Grover, M. B. "Dealing with Daddy Stress." *Forbes,* Sept. 6, 1999, pp. 202–208.

Hansen, L. S. *Integrative Life Planning: Critical Tasks for Career Development and Changing Life Patterns.* San Francisco: Jossey-Bass, 1997.

Joyce, A. "Other Ways to Make a Job Pay." *Washington Post,* Mar. 1, 1999, p. F09.

Kaplan, R. E. *SKILLSCOPE.* Greensboro, N.C.: Center for Creative Leadership, 1997.

Kaplan, R. E., Drath, W. H., and Kofodimos, J. R. *Beyond Ambition: How Driven Managers Can Lead Better and Live Better.* San Francisco: Jossey-Bass, 1991.

Koehn, N. F. "Estee Lauder: Self-Definition and the Modern Cosmetics Market." In P. Scranton (ed.), *Beauty and Business.* New York: Routledge, 2000.

Kofodimos, J. R. *Balancing Act: How Managers Can Integrate Successful Careers and Fulfilling Personal Lives.* San Francisco: Jossey-Bass, 1993.

Kundera, M. *The Unbearable Lightness of Being.* New York: HarperCollins, 1984.

Leibovich, M. "AOL's Steve Case, the Internet's 'Premiere CEO.'" *Detroit News,* Nov. 26, 1998, pp. 3, 19.

Leider, R. J. "The Ultimate Leadership Task: Self-Leadership." In F. Hesselbein, M. Goldsmith, and R. Beckhard (eds.), *The Leader of the Future: New Visions, Strategies, and Practices for the Next Era.* San Francisco: Jossey-Bass, 1996.

Leider, R. J. *The Power of Purpose.* San Francisco: Berrett-Koehler, 1997.

Leider, R. J. "Are You Deciding on Purpose?" *Fast Company,* Feb.-Mar. 1998, pp. 114–116.

Levine, J. *Working Fathers: New Strategies for Balancing Work and Family.* Reading, Mass.: Addison-Wesley, 1997.

Levine, S. B. *Father Courage: What Happens When Men Put Family First.* Orlando, Fla.: Harcourt Brace, 2000.

Lombardo, M. M., and Eichinger, R. W. *Eighty-Eight Assignments for Development in Place: Enhancing the Developmental Challenge of Existing Jobs.* Greensboro, N.C.: Center for Creative Leadership, 1989.

Lombardo, M. M., McCall, M. W., and Morrison, A. M. *The Lessons of Experience: How Successful Executives Develop on the Job.* San Francisco: New Lexington Books, 1988.

Lombardo, M. M., and McCauley, C. D. *Benchmarks.* Greensboro, N.C.: Center for Creative Leadership, 2000.

Manske, F. *Secrets of Effective Leadership.* Memphis, Tenn.: Leadership Education and Development, 1987.

McCauley, C. D., and Douglas, C. A. "Developmental Relationships." In C. D. McCauley, R. Moxley, and E. Van Velsor (eds.), *The Center for Creative Leadership Handbook of Leadership Development.* San Francisco: Jossey-Bass, 1998.

Miller, D. "The Future Organization: A Chameleon in All Its Glory." In F. Hesselbein, M. Goldsmith, and R. Beckhard (eds.), *The Organization of the Future.* San Francisco: Jossey-Bass, 1997.

Noer, D. *Breaking Free: A Prescription for Personal and Organizational Change.* San Francisco: Jossey-Bass, 1997.

Reitzes, D. C., and Mutran, E. J. "Multiple Roles and Identities: Factors Influencing Self-Esteem Among Middle-Aged Working Men and Women." *Social Psychology Quarterly,* 1994, *57*(4), 313–325.

Ruderman, M. N., Ohlott, P. J., Panzer, K., and King, S. N. "Psychological and Professional Benefits of Multiple Roles for Managerial Women." Unpublished manuscript, 1999.

Sacks, O. *The Man Who Mistook His Wife for a Hat.* New York: Simon & Schuster, 1970.

Senge, P. M. *The Fifth Discipline: The Art and Practice of the Learning Organization.* New York: Doubleday, 1990.

Sessa, V. I. "Can Conflict Improve Team Effectiveness?" *Issues and Observations,* 1994, *14*(4), 1–5.

Stacks, J. F. "The Powell Factor." *Time Magazine, 146*(2), July 10, 1995, p. 22.

Vaill, P. B. *Managing as a Performing Art: New Ideas for a World of Chaotic Change.* San Francisco: Jossey-Bass, 1989.

Wilhelm, W. "Learning from Past Leaders." In F. Hesselbein, M. Goldsmith, and R. Beckhard (eds.), *The Leader of the Future: New Visions, Strategies, and Practices for the Next Era.* San Francisco: Jossey-Bass, 1996.

INDEX

A

Achievement, 60

Action tactics, 90–91. *See also* Learning styles

Activity, 60

Advancement, 60

Adventure, 60

Aesthetics, 60

Affiliation, 60

Affluence, 60

Age, 130–131

Agility, 81. *See also* Competencies, leadership

Alliances, creating, 80–81. *See also* Competencies, leadership

Allied Signal, 56

Ambiguity, 81. *See also* Competencies, leadership

America Online (AOL), 40

AOL Time Warner, 40

Arden, E., 35

Artist's Way, The (Cameron), 47

Arts & Entertainment Network, 35, 36

Associated Consultants in Education, 158

Authenticity: and example of Estee Lauder, 35–36; and leadership vision, 34

Authority, dispersal of, 18–19, 60

Autonomy, 60

B

Baby bust generation. *See* Generation X

B

Balance: in framework for examining leadership role, 10; and impact of personal lives on work, 105–106; and impact of work on personal lives, 105; importance of, to leadership, 101–105; organizational preference for, 104; and parenting, 108–110; and performance, 10; and tension between mastery and intimacy, 107–108; as value, 60

Balance, achievement of: adding resources for, 117; integrating strategy for, 111–113; moderating strategy for, 115–116; narrowing strategy for, 114–115; and rechecking of values, 110–111; sequencing strategy for, 116–117

Balancing Act (Kofodimos), 107–108

Bell ringers, 138–140

Ben & Jerry's Homemade, Inc., 57

Ben and Jerry's Double Dip: Lead with Your Values and Make Money Too (Cohen and Greenfield), 58

Benchmarks (Lombardo and McCauley), 103

Bennis, W. G., 88

Brown, T., 73

Bunker, K. A., 94

C

Calling view of leadership, 23

Cameron, J., 47

Campbell, D., 85, 87

Campbell Leadership Index, 85

Careers: and career change, 132–133; and career choices, 33–34; and career history, 96–99; changing, and employee relations, 19; four necessities for, 66

Caretaking: and costs of leadership, 27; roles, 122–125

Carlson Learning Company, 159

Case, S., 40

Cashman, K., 11, 73

Center for Creative Leadership, 8, 88, 89, 94, 96, 103, 105, 153, 157

Challenge, 60, 88–92. *See also* Learning styles

Change: BSer response to, 95; as cause of stress, 92–93; entrenched response to, 95; integration of, with continuity, 93; learner response to, 95–96; overwhelmed response to, 94–95; resistance to, 93–94; as value, 60

Change Agent Questionnaire (Teleometrics International), 157

Characteristics, personal, 85–88. *See also* Self-awareness

Charland, W., 133

Cheerleaders, 150

Clarity, of personal vision, 36–49

Cohen, B., 57, 58

Cohorts, 150

Collaboration, 60

Communication, 82. *See also* Competencies, leadership

Community, 60

Competencies, leadership, 80–83

Competency, 60

Competition, 60

Comprehensive Leader, The: A New View of Visionary Leadership (inventory tool), 158

Conflict: responses to, 46; value of, in careers, 66–69

Conger, J. A., 21

Congruence, determination of, 62–65

Consulting Psychologists Press, 159

Context, changing, in examining leadership role, 10

Cooper, G., 22

Core values: change in, over time, 65; conflicts, incompatibilities, and, 63–65; and congruence, 62–65; definition of personal, 59–62; identification of, 58–65; matching, with action, 63. *See also* Leadership values; Values

Counseling, 149–150

Courage, 60

Couric, K., 43, 44

Covey, S. R., 112

Creativity, 47, 58, 60

Customer focus, hierarchies *versus*, 18–19

D

Dalton, M. A., 89

Daydreams, 39–41

"Dealing with Daddy Stress" *(Forbes)*, 109

Demands, changing, in examining leadership role, 10

Diversity, 60

Douglas, C. A., 149, 150

Drath, W. H., 73–74, 79

Drift, 3; problem of, 4–7; turning, into conscious choices, 8

Drucker, P. F., 18, 19

Duty, 60

E

Economic security, 60

Effectiveness. *See* Power, definition of

Eichinger, R. W., 88

Eighty-Eight Assignments for Development in Place (Lombardo and Eichinger), 88

Emotional strain, and costs of leadership, 27

Emotional support, from balanced work and personal lives, 106

Employee relations, and changing careers, 19

Energies, investment of, 43

Enjoyment, 60
Equality, 58
Esquire magazine, 44
Estee Lauder Companies, Inc., 35
European Enlightenment, 40
Executive Profile Survey (IPAT), 158
Expectations, moderation of, 115–116
Expertise, dispersal of, 18–19

F

Fame, 60
Family: strains on, 28; as value, 60
Family and Medical Leave Act (1993), 110
Father Courage: What Happens When Men Put Family First (Levine), 109
Feedback, less supportive, and costs of leadership, 28–29
Feeling tactics, 90–91. *See also* Learning styles
Finian's Rainbow (Broadway musical), 40
Flexibility, 81. *See also* Competencies, leadership
Focus, 42–43
Forbes magazine, 109
Freedom of expression, and costs of leadership, 28
Friends, 125–126
Fulfillment, versus function, in leaders, 3
Fun, 58

G

Gandhi, M., 40
Gates, W., 43, 44
Generation X, 19, 77, 101, 110
Generation Y, 110
Generational changes, 19–20
Genetic view of leadership, 22
Greenfield, J., 57, 58
Grover, M. B., 109

H

Hambrecht & Quist, 40
Hansen, L. S., 19, 113, 132, 133
Health, 60, 129–130

Hierarchies, customer focus versus, 18–19
Helping others, as value, 60
Heroism, 22
HRD Press, 158
HRDQ, 158
Human Synergistic, Inc., 159
Humor, 60

I

Imagination, 38
Imbalance, spiral of, 107
Impact. *See* Power, definition of
Impact, personal, 77–78
Influence. *See* Power, definition of
Inner harmony, 60
Insight Inventory (HRD), 158
Integration, 111–113. *See also* Balance, achievement of
Integrative Life Planning (Hansen), 113
Integrity, 60
Interpersonal skills, 105
Intimacy, mastery versus, 107–108
Intuition, 47–48
Involvement, creative, 47
IPAT, 158

J

Jefferson, T., 40
Job insecurity, and costs of leadership, 28
Joyce, A., 77, 102
Justice, 61

K

Kaplan, R. E., 73–74, 103
Kennedy, J. F., 19
Kennedy, R. F., 19
Kimsey, J., 40
King, M. L., Jr., 19, 40
King, S. N., 103, 105
Knowledge, 61
Koehn, N. F., 35, 133

Kofodimus, J. R., 73–74
Kundera, M., 53

L

Lauder, E., 35, 36, 133
Lauder, J., 133
Leaders: differing expectations of, 25
Leadership: benefits of, 140–143; competencies for, 80–83; costs of, 26–29, 140–143; expanding views and images of, 21–26; heroic view of, 22; importance of balance to, 101–105; learned view of, 22; personal vision view of, 25–26; position view of, 23; resources for, 155–157; results of differing views of, 24–25; roles, 83–85; top-only view of, 22; as vocation, 6; what changes in organizations mean for, 20–21
Leadership, role of: attaining of, through drift, 3–4; examination of, as ongoing process, 9–11; five significant areas for examining, 9–11; framework for examining, 10, 136, 137; and leadership outside of work, 9; and problem of drift, 4–7; and turning drift into conscious choices, 8–9
Leadership decision ladder, 143–147
Leadership motivation: and meaning, 79; and personal validation, 76; and rewards, 76–77; sources of, 75–79; in terms of service, 78–79; and urge to have impact, 77–78
Leadership Resources: A Guide to Training and Development Tools (Schwartz, Axtman, and Freeman), 157
Leadership values: appropriateness of, 57–58; basing, on personal values, 55–69. *See also* Core values; Values
Leadership vision: articulation of, 33; definition of, 31; and example of Estee Lauder, 35–36; grounding of, in personal vision, 34; questions for crafting of personal, 50–53
Leadership/Personality Compatibility Inventory (L/PCI), 158

Learning, capacity for, 88–92
Learning styles, 88–92
Leibovich, M., 40
Leider, R. J., 7, 71, 75, 76
Levine, J., 109, 110
Levine, S. B., 109
Life plan, 33
Life Styles Inventory (Human Synergistic, Inc.), 158–159
Lincoln Memorial, 40
Location: geographic, importance of, 128–129; as value, 61
Lombardo, M. M., 88, 96, 103
Long Island, New York, 57
Love, 61
Loyalty, 61

M

Managerial Work-Values Scale, 159
Mandela, N., 43, 44
Manske, F., 31
Marcus, S., 35
Mastery, versus intimacy, 107–108
McCall, M. W., 88, 96
McCauley, C. D., 103, 149, 150
Meaning, 79
Mentors, 150–151
Mentzer, J. E., 35. *See also* Lauder, E.
Miller, D., 18
Moderating strategy, 115–116. *See also* Balance, achievement of
Morrison, A. M., 88, 96
Motivation. *See* Leadership motivation
Multiple roles, commitment to, 103–104
Multiple tasks, handling, 106
Mutran, E. J., 114
Myth, 38

N

Nanus, B., 88
Narrative, personal, 37–39

Narrowing, 114–115. *See also* Balance, achievement of

Neiman-Marcus, 35

Networks, creating, 80–81. *See also* Competencies, leadership

Noer, D., 94, 95

Noglows, P., 40

O

Ohlott, P. J., 103, 105

Order, 61

Organizations: changing careers and employee relations in, 19; as contexts in which to envision leadership, 17; and generational changes, 19–20; from hierarchies to customer focus in, 18–19; major changes in, 18–20

P

Palus, C. J., 79

Panzer, K., 103, 105

Parenting, 108–110

Partitioning, integration versus, 112–113

Patterns, behavioral, 41–43, 137–138

Perfection, 101

Personal commitments, overview of, 118–127

Personal development, 61

Personal lives: impact of, on work, 105–106; impact of work on, 105

Personal Profile System (Carlson Learning Company), 159

Personal Strengths Publishing, Inc., 159

Personal vision: articulation of, 33–34; clarity of, 36–49; connection of, to leadership, 31–36; and creative involvement, 47; daydreams and, 39–41; definition of, 31; and discovery of patterns, 41–43; effects of, 32–33; Estee Lauder, as example of, 35–36; and feelings about power, 45; and intuition, 47–48; and personal narrative, 37–39; and responses to conflict, 46; role models and, 43–44; as useful guide, 33; ways to clarify, 37

Physical fitness, 61

Powell, C., 23

Power: decentralization of, 18–19; definition of, 45

Power Base Inventory (Consulting Psychologists Press), 159

Power of Purpose, The (Leider), 7

Predictability, 43

Primary relationship, 121–122

Program participant questionnaire, 153–154

Psychological benefits, of balanced work and personal life, 106

Public duties, and costs of leadership, 27

Purpose, sense of, 36

Q

Quality, 58

Queens, New York, 35

R

Recognition, 61

Reitzes, D. C., 114

Relief, infrequent, 28

Resources, adding, 117

Responsibility, 61

Rewards, 76–77

Role models, 43–44

Roles: accumulation of, 114–115; and caretaking, 122–125; and friends, 125–126; in groups, 41–43; and personal commitments, 118–121; and primary relationship, 121–122; and volunteer work, 126–127

Rubenstein, H., 35

Ruderman, M. N., 103, 105

S

Sacks, O., 37

San Francisco, California, 40

Secrets of Effective Leadership (Manske), 31

Self-assessments, instruments for, 157–159

Self-awareness: areas of, 75; and capacity to learn, 88–92; in framework for examining leadership role, 10; importance of, to leadership, 72–74; and lessons learned from career history, 96–99; and motivation to lead, 75–79; and personal characteristics, 85–88; and personal leadership profile, 74–75; and responses to change, 92–96

Self-image, 41–43

Self-respect, 61

Senge, P. M., 24

Separation, and costs of leadership, 27

Sequencing, 116–117. *See also* Balance, achievement of

Service, 78–79

Sessa, V. I., 46

Seven Habits of Highly Effective People, The (Covey), 112

Silent Generation, 20

SKILLSCOPE questionnaire (Kaplan), 103

Social responsibility, 58

Social script view of leadership, 22

Sounding board, 149

Spirituality, 61

Sports, early leadership stories in, 38

Stacks, J. F., 23

Stamina, and costs of leadership, 27

Status, 61

Stewart, J., 22

Story, personal. *See* Narrative, personal

Strategic vision, creating, 82. *See also* Competencies, leadership

Strength Deployment Inventory (Personal Strengths Publishing, Inc.), 159

T

Teams, building, 80. *See also* Competencies, leadership

Technical savvy, 81. *See also* Competencies, leadership

Teleometric International, 157

Themes, recurring, 39, 137–138. *See also* Narrative, personal

Thinking tactics, 90–91. *See also* Learning styles

Three Mile Island, 19

Today show (television), 44

Top-only view of leadership, 22

Trade-offs, 34

Traits, personal, 35–36

Trust, building, 80. *See also* Competencies, leadership

U

Unbearable Lightness of Being (Kundera), 53

Uncertainty, 81. *See also* Competencies, leadership

V

Vaill, P. B., 72

Validation, personal, 76

Values: and balance, 110–111; and behavior, 55–58; clarity about, 56–57; conflicts of, in careers, 66–69; definition of, 55; in framework for examining leadership role, 10. *See also* Core values

Variation, 60

Visibility, and costs of leadership, 26–27

Vision: as beginning of effectiveness in leadership, 31–32; in framework for examining leadership role, 10. *See also* Leadership vision; Personal vision

Vocation, choice of, 33–34

Volunteer work, 126–127

W

Watergate, 19

Wayne, J., 22

Wilhelm, W., 56

Wisdom, 61

Work: impact of, on personal lives, 105–106; impact of personal lives on, 105

Working Fathers: New Strategies for Balancing Work and Family (Levine), 109, 110

More Titles from the <u>Center for Creative Leadership</u>

Leadership in Action
Martin Wilcox, Editor

Keep yourself up to date on the latest research, findings, strategies, and practices impacting leadership today. *Leadership in Action* offers readers the latest insights from CCL's many ongoing research projects and expert advice on how its findings can best be applied in the real world. Published bimonthly, each issue of this cutting-edge journal delivers in-depth articles designed to help practicing leaders hone their existing skills and identify and develop new ones.

One year (six issues) individual rate: $99.00
One year (six issues) institutional rate: $124.00

Maximizing the Value of 360-Degree Feedback
A Process for Successful Individual and Organizational Development
Walter Tornow, Manuel London, & CCL Associates

In this unprecedented volume, CCL draws upon twenty-eight years of leading research and professional experience to deliver the most thorough, practical, and accessible guide to 360-degree feedback ever. Readers will discover precisely how they can use 360-degree feedback as a tool for achieving a variety of objectives such as communicating performance expectations, setting developmental goals, establishing a learning culture, and tracking the effects of organizational change. Detailed guidelines show how 360-degree feedback can be designed to maximize employee involvement, self-determination, and commitment. Filled with case examples and a full complement of instructive instruments.

Hardcover   320 pages   Item #F093 $42.95

"This wonderfully useful guide to leadership development will prove an invaluable resource to anyone interested in growing the talent of their organizations."—Jay A. Conger, professor, USC, and author of *Learning to Lead*

The Center for Creative Leadership
Handbook of Leadership Development
Cynthia D. McCauley, Russ S. Moxley,
Ellen Van Velsor, Editors

In one comprehensive volume, the Center for Creative Leadership distills its philosophy, findings, and methodologies into a practical resource that sets a new standard in the field. Filled with proven techniques and detailed instructions for designing and enabling the most effective leadership development programs possible—including six developed by CCL itself—this is the ultimate professional guide from the most prestigious organization in the field.

Hardcover   512 pages   Item #F116 $65.00

"At last, a practical, quick, direct, and easy-to-use tool that helps individuals flex their learning muscles! I'll use the Learning Tactics Inventory (LTI) in my consulting practice right away."
—Beverly Kaye, author, *Up Is Not the Only Way*

Learning Tactics Inventory
Facilitator's Guide & Participant's Workbook
Maxine Dalton

Developed by CCL, the Learning Tactics Inventory (LTI) gives you everything you need to conduct a two- to four-hour workshop that dramatically enhances participants' ability to learn by showing each individual how he or she learns best and how each can adopt new learning strategies accordingly. The *Inventory* is used by workshop participants to profile individual learning styles. The *Participant's Workbook* is used to score and interpret results. The *Facilitator's Guide*, which includes a sample copy of the *Participant's Workbook*, details all key workshop procedures—including setup, administration, and follow-up—and comes with reproducible overhead and handout masters. You'll need one Inventory and Workbook per participant. Available at bulk discounts.

LTI Inventory   paperback   48 pages   Item #G515 $12.95
LTI Facilitator's Guide [includes sample Workbook]   paperback   48 pages   Item #G514 $24.95

Job Challenge Profile
Learning from Work Experience
Marian N. Ruderman, Cynthia D. McCauley,
Patricia J. Ohlott

Increase career satisfaction and job performance among your employees with these field-tested tools that help them seek new challenges and develop valuable new skills in the course of their professional lives. The *Inventory* will help them profile what and how much they're learning, where their key challenges lie, and how they can maximize learning in their day-to-day experiences. The *Participant's Workbook* is used to score and interpret results. The *Facilitator's Guide*, which includes a sample copy of the *Participant's Workbook*, contains complete instructions for conducting two- to four-hour workshops. The result will be the creation of a learning work environment where challenge is welcome and job fulfillment runs high.

JCP Instrument   6 pages   Item #G108 $4.95
JCP Participant's Workbook   paperback   48 pages   Item #G106 $12.95
JCP Facilitator's Guide [includes sample Workbook]   paperback
48 pages   Item #G107 $24.95

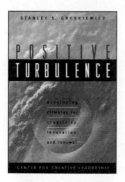

Positive Turbulence
Developing Climates for Creativity, Innovation, and Renewal
Stanley S. Gryskiewicz

Can your company manage—even encourage—turbulence in ways that actually strengthen its competitive stance? Absolutely. In this work, top organizational psychologist Stanley Gryskiewicz argues that challenges to the status quo can be catalysts for creativity, innovation, and renewal and shows leaders how they can keep their company on the competitive edge by embracing a process he calls Positive Turbulence. Developed through the author's work with many of the world's leading companies over the course of thirty years, *Positive Turbulence* delivers proven methods for creating an organization that continuously renews itself through the committed pursuit of new ideas, products, and processes.

Hardcover   224 pages   Item #E952 $32.95

Leadership and Spirit
Breathing New Vitality and Energy into Individuals and Organizations
Russ S. Moxley

Learn how you can harness your inner spirit to help yourself and those around you approach work with a renewed sense of purpose and satisfaction. In this book, Moxley shows how spirit can spawn a more vital and vibrant kind of leadership—one that, in turn, promotes the creativity, vitality, and well-being of others. Here, Moxley examines various leadership practices: those that elevate people's spirits and those that cause the spirit to wither and wane. He offers specific suggestions on what each of us can do to reach a new level of awareness regarding leadership. And he demonstrates how a spirited leadership that values rituals, celebrations, and employee input creates a totally engaged workforce; one that brings the whole person—mental, emotional, physical, *and* spiritual—to work.

Hardcover   256 pages   ISBN 0-7879-0949-1   Item #F115-3C9 $30.95

Executive Selection
Strategies for Success
Valerie I. Sessa, Jodi J. Taylor

As evinced by recent crises at Aetna, Mattel, and Citicorp, a single misstep in selecting top executives can spell trouble for the most stable of organizations. Yet the development of clear criteria for executive selection is too often pushed aside in the face of more immediate challenges. Based on Center for Creative Leadership research and the authors' extensive experience in dealing with top-level executives, this book outlines a comprehensive system for matching the right person with the right job. By answering such questions as "Who should be involved in the hiring decision?" and "How can the best candidates be identified?" this book will help ensure that your organization always enjoys quality leadership.

Hardcover   208 pages   ISBN 0-7879-5020-3   Item #G700 $34.95

Available in Bookstores or Call Toll Free 1-800-956-7739
or Visit Our Web Site at www.jbp.com

 Jossey-Bass
350 Sansome Street
San Francisco, CA 94104